SOUTHERN GHOSTS

Scarifying True Tales
from the Old South

HANS HOLZER

Tess
Press

Published by Tess Press,
an imprint of Black Dog & Leventhal Publishers, Inc.
151 West 19th Street
New York, NY 10011

Designed by Tony Meisel

Cover design by Filip Zawodnik

Cover photo courtesy of The Civil War and
Underground Railroad Museum of Philadelphia

Printed in the United States of America

ISBN-10: 1-57912-424-0/ISBN-13: 978-1-57912-424-3

d f g e c

CONTENTS

PUBLISHER'S NOTE

WELCOME TO THE HAUNTED SOUTH. There is something about Dixie's history; the antebellum mansions, the love of story-telling, and the fascination with genealogy that has fostered some of the best and spookiest stories in the world.

This evocative and bone-chilling collection of stories captures the excitement of ghost-hunting and identification south of the Mason-Dixon line. The ghosts you will encounter are not figments of overactive imaginations, they are human personalities—people who have died traumatically, usually tragically, who are unaware of their own deaths. Professor Hans Holzer is a renowned parapsychologist who has visited each of the sites in the book and, with the help of psychic Sybil Leek, has identified the ghost in residence by sights, sounds, poltergeist activities, dream visions, and other experiences that signal the presence of someone from "the other side."

According to Professor Holzer the slower, more tradition-bound atmosphere of the southern states tends to encourage a pre-occupation with the occult. The personal attitude of many Southerners toward the unseen differs sharply from that of the Northerner. In the South, if the story is romantic and interesting, it merits retelling, from generation to generation.

So proceed if you dare—into the past that haunts the present in the pages of *Southern Ghosts*.

> *"Time does not pass very fast in Dixie,*
> *nor does memory ever fade."*
> – Professor Hans Holzer

1. MICHIE TAVERN, JEFFERSON, AND THE BOYS

"THIS TYPICAL PRE-REVOLUTIONARY TAVERN was a favorite stopping place for travelers," the official guide to Charlottesville says. "With its colonial furniture and china, its beamed and paneled rooms, it appears much the way it did in the days when Jefferson and Monroe were visitors. Monroe writes of entertaining Lafayette as his guest at dinner here, and General Andrew Jackson, fresh from his victory at New Orleans, stopped over on his way to Washington."

The guide, however, does not mention that the tavern was moved a considerable distance from its original place to a much more accessible location where the tourist trade could benefit from it more. Regardless of this comparatively recent change of position, the tavern is exactly as it was, with everything inside, including its ghosts, intact. At the original site, it was surrounded by trees which framed it and sometimes towered over it. At the new site, facing the road, it looks out into the Virginia countryside almost like a manor house. One walks up to the wooden structure over a number of steps and enters the old tavern to the left or, if one prefers, the pub to the right, which is nowadays a coffee shop. Taverns in the eighteenth and early nineteenth centuries were not simply bars or inns;

they were meeting places where people could talk freely, some-times about political subjects. They were used as headquarters for Revolutionary movements or for invading military forces. Most taverns of any size had ballrooms in which the social functions of the area could be held. Only a few private individuals were wealthy enough to have their own ballrooms built into their manor houses.

What is fortunate about Michie Tavern is the fact that every-thing is pretty much as it was in the eighteenth century, and what-ever restorations have been undertaken are completely authentic. The furniture and cooking utensils, the tools of the innkeeper, the porcelain, the china, the metal objects are all of the period, whether they had been in the house or not. As is customary with historical restorations or preservations, whatever is missing in the house is supplied by painstaking historical research, and objects of the same period and the same area are substituted for those presumably lost during the intervening period.

The tavern has three floors and a large number of rooms, so we would need the two hours we had allowed ourselves for the visit. After looking at the downstairs part of the tavern, with its "com-mon" kitchen and the over-long wooden table where two dozen people could be fed, we mounted the stairs to the second floor.

Ingrid, the medium, kept looking into various rooms, sniffing out the psychic presences, as it were, while I followed close behind. Horace Burr and Virginia Cloud kept a respectable distance, as if trying not to "frighten" the ghosts away. That was all right with me, because I did not want Ingrid to tap the unconscious of either one of these very knowledgeable people.

Finally we arrived in the third-floor ballroom of the old tavern.

I asked Ingrid what she had felt in the various rooms below. "In the pink room on the second floor I felt an argument or some sort of strife but nothing special in any of the other rooms."

"What about this big ballroom?"

"I can see a lot of people around here. There is a gay atmosphere, and I think important people came here; it is rather exclusive, this room. I think it was used just on special occasions."

By now I had waved Horace and Virginia to come closer, since it had become obvious to me that they wanted very much to hear what Ingrid was saying. Possibly new material might come to light, unknown to both of these historians, in which case they might verify it later on or comment upon it on the spot.

"I'm impressed with an argument over a woman here," Ingrid continued. "It has to do with one of the dignitaries, and it is about one of their wives."

"How does the argument end?"

"I think they just had a quick argument here, about her infidelity."

"Who are the people involved?"

"I think Hamilton. I don't know the woman's name."

"Who is the other man?"

"I think Jefferson was here."

"Try to get as much of the argument as you can."

Ingrid closed her eyes, sat down in a chair generally off limits to visitors, and tried to tune in on the past. "I get the argument as a real embarrassment," she began. "The woman is frail, she has a long dress on with lace at the top part around the neck, her hair is light brown."

"Does she take part in the argument?"

"Yes, she has to side with her husband."

"Describe her husband."

"I can't see his face, but he is dressed in a brocade jacket pulled back with buttons down the front and breeches. It is a very fancy outfit."

"How does it all end?"

"Well, nothing more is said. It is just a terrible embarrassment."

"Is this some sort of special occasion? Are there other people here?"

"Yes, oh, yes. It is like an anniversary or something of that sort. Perhaps a political anniversary of some kind. There is music and dancing and candlelight."

While Ingrid was speaking, in an almost inaudible voice, Horace and Virginia were straining to hear what she was saying but not being very successful at it. At this point Horace waved to me, and I tiptoed over to him.

"Ask her to get the period a little closer," he whispered in my ear.

I went back to Ingrid and put the question to her. "I think it was toward the end of the war," she said, "toward the very end of it. For some time now I've had the figure 1781 impressed on my mind."

Since nothing further seemed to be forthcoming from Ingrid at this point, I asked her to relax and come back to the present, so that we could discuss her impressions freely.

"The name Hamilton is impossible in this connection," Horace Burr began. But I was quick to interject that the name Hamilton was fairly common in the late eighteenth and early nineteenth centuries and that Ingrid need not have referred to the Alexander Hamilton. "Jefferson was here many times, and he could have been involved in this," Burr continued. "I think I know who the other man might have been. But could we, just for once, try questioning the medium on specific issues?"

Neither Ingrid nor I objected, and Horace proceeded to ask Ingrid to identify the couple she had felt in the ballroom. Ingrid threw her head back for a moment, closed her eyes, and then replied, "The man is very prominent in politics, one of the big three or four at the time, and one of the reasons this is all so embarrassing, from what I get, is that the other man is of much lower caliber. He is not one of the big leaders; he may be an officer or something like that."

While Ingrid was speaking, slowly, as it were, I again felt the strange sense of transportation, of looking back in time, which had been coming to me more and more often recently, always unsought and usually only of fleeting duration. "For what it is worth," I said, "while Ingrid is speaking, I also get a very vague impression that all this has something to do with two sisters. It concerns a rivalry between two sisters."

"The man's outfit," Ingrid continued her narrative, "was sort of gold and white brocade and very fancy. He was the husband. I don't see the other man."

Horace seemed unusually agitated at this. "Tell me, did this couple live in this vicinity or did they come from far away on a special anniversary?"

"They lived in the vicinity and came just for the evening."

"Well, Horace?" I said, getting more and more curious, since he was apparently driving in a specific direction. "What was this all about?"

For once, Horace enjoyed being the center of attraction. "Well, it was a hot and heavy situation, all right. The couple were Mr. and Mrs. John Walker—he was the son of Dr. Walker of Castle Hill. And the man, who wasn't here, was Jefferson himself. Ingrid is right in saying that they lived in the vicinity—Castle Hill is not far away from here."

"But what about the special festivity that brought them all together here?"

Horace wasn't sure what it could have been, but Virginia, in great excitement, broke in. "It was in this room that the waltz was danced for the first time in America. A young man had come from France dressed in very fancy clothes. The lady he danced with was a closely chaperoned girl from Charlottesville. She was very young, and she danced the waltz with this young man, and everybody in Charlottesville was shocked. The news went around town that the young lady had danced with a man holding her, and that was just terrible at the time. Perhaps that was the occasion. Michie Tavern was a stopover for stagecoaches, and Jefferson and the local people would meet here to get their news. Downstairs was the meeting room, but up here in the ballroom the more special events took place, such as the introduction of the waltz."

I turned to Horace Burr. "How is it that this tavern no longer stands on the original site? I understand it has been moved here for easier tourist access."

"Yes," Horace replied. "The building originally stood near the airport. In fact, the present airport is on part of the old estate that belonged to Colonel John Henry, the father of Patrick Henry. Young Patrick spent part of his boyhood there. Later, Colonel Henry sold the land to the Michies. This house was then their main house. It was on the old highway. In turn, they built themselves an elaborate mansion which is still standing and turned this house into a tavern. All the events we have been discussing took place while this building was on the old site. In 1926 it was moved here.

Originally, I think the ballroom we are standing in now was just the loft of the old Henry house. They raised part of the roof to make it into a ballroom because they had no meeting room in the tavern."

In the attractively furnished coffee shop to the right of the main tavern, Mrs. Juanita Godfrey, the manager, served us steaming hot black coffee and sat down to chat with us. Had anyone ever complained about unusual noises or other inexplicable manifestations in the tavern? I asked.

"Some of the employees who work here at night do hear certain sounds they can't account for," Mrs. Godfrey replied. "They will hear something and go and look, and there will be nothing there."

"In what part of the building?"

"All over, even in this area. This is a section of the slave quarters, and it is very old."

Mrs. Godfrey did not seem too keen on psychic experiences, I felt. To the best of her knowledge, no one had had any unusual experiences in the tavern. "What about the lady who slept here one night?" I inquired.

"You mean Mrs. Milton—yes, she slept here one night." But Mrs. Godfrey knew nothing of Mrs. Milton's experiences.

However, Virginia had met the lady, who was connected with the historical preservation effort of the community. "One night when Mrs. Milton was out of town," Virginia explained, "I slept in her room. At the time she confessed to me that she had heard footsteps frequently, especially on the stairway down."

"That is the area she slept in, yes," Mrs. Godfrey confirmed. "She slept in the ladies' parlor on the first floor."

"What about yourself, Virginia? Did you hear anything?"

"I heard noises, but the wood sometimes behaves very funny. She, however, said they were definitely footsteps. That was in 1961."

What had Ingrid unearthed in the ballroom of Michie Tavern? Was it merely the lingering imprint of America's first waltz, scandalous to the early Americans but innocent in the light of today? Or was it something more—an involvement between Mrs. Walker and the illustrious Thomas Jefferson? My image of the great American had always been that of a man above human frailties. But my eyes were to be opened still further on a most intriguing visit to Monticello, Jefferson's home.

2. A VISIT WITH THE SPIRITED JEFFERSON

"YOU'RE WELCOME TO VISIT MONTICELLO to continue the parapsychological research which you are conducting relative to the personalities of 1776," wrote James A. Bear, Jr., of the Thomas Jefferson Memorial Foundation, and he arranged for us to go to the popular tourist attraction after regular hours, to permit Ingrid the peace and tranquility necessary to tune in on the very fragile vibrations that might hang on from the past.

Jefferson, along with Benjamin Franklin, is a widely popular historical figure: a play, a musical, and a musical film have brought him to life, showing him as the shy, dedicated, intellectual architect of the Declaration of Independence. Jefferson, the gentle Virginia farmer, the man who wants to free the slaves but is thwarted in his efforts by other Southerners; Jefferson, the ardent but bashful lover of his wife; Jefferson, the ideal of virtue and American patriotism—these are the images put across by the entertainment media, by countless books, and by the tourist authorities who try to entice visitors to come to Charlottesville and visit Jefferson's home, Monticello.

Even the German tourist service plugged itself into the Jefferson boom. "This is like a second mother country for me,"

Thomas Jefferson is quoted as saying while traveling down the Rhine. "Everything that isn't English in our country comes from here." Jefferson compared the German Rhineland to certain portions of Maryland and Pennsylvania and pointed out that the second largest ethnic group in America at that time were Germans. In an article in the German language weekly Aufbau, Jefferson is described as the first prominent American tourist in the Rhineland. His visit took place in April 1788. At the time Jefferson was ambassador to Paris, and the Rhine journey allowed him to study agriculture, customs, and conditions on both sides of the Rhine. Unquestionably, Jefferson, along with Washington, Franklin, and Lincoln, represents one of the pillars of the American edifice. Virginia Cloud, ever the avid historian of her area, points out that not only did Jefferson and John Adams have a close relationship as friends and political contemporaries but there were certain uncanny "coincidences" between their lives. For instance, Jefferson and Adams died within hours of each other, Jefferson in Virginia and Adams in Massachusetts, on July 4, 1826—exactly fifty years to the day they had both signed the Declaration of Independence. Adams's last words were, "But Jefferson still lives." At the time that was no longer true, for Jefferson had died earlier in the day.

Jefferson's imprint is all over Charlottesville. Not only did the talented "Renaissance man" design his own home, Monticello, but he also designed the Rotunda, the focal point of the University of Virginia. Jefferson, Madison, and Monroe were members of the first governing board of the University, which is now famous for its school of medicine—and which, incidentally, is the leading university in the study of parapsychology, since Dr. Ian Stevenson teaches there.

On our way to Monticello we decided to visit the old Swan

Tavern, which had some important links to Jefferson. The tavern is now used as a private club, but the directors graciously allowed us to come in, even the ladies, who are generally not admitted. Nothing in the furnishings reminds one of the old tavern, since the place has been extensively remodeled to suit the requirements of the private club. At first we inspected the downstairs and smiled at several elderly gentlemen who hadn't the slightest idea why we were there. Then we went to the upper story and finally came to rest in a room to the rear of the building. As soon as Ingrid had seated herself in a comfortable chair in a corner, I closed the door and asked her what she felt about this place, of which she had no knowledge.

"I feel that people came here to talk things over in a lighter vein, perhaps over a few drinks."

"Was there anyone in particular who was outstanding among these people?"

"I keep thinking of Jefferson, and I'm seeing big mugs; most of the men have big mugs in front of them."

Considering that Ingrid did not know the past of the building as a tavern, this was pretty evidential. I asked her about Jefferson.

"I think he was the figurehead. This matter concerned him greatly, but I don't think it had anything to do with his own wealth or anything like that."

"At the time when this happened, was there a warlike action in progress?"

"Yes, I think it was on the outskirts of town. I have the feeling that somebody was trying to reach this place and that they were waiting for somebody, and yet they weren't really expecting that person."

Both Horace Burr and Virginia Cloud were visibly excited that

Ingrid had put her finger on it, so to speak. Virginia had been championing the cause of the man about whom Ingrid had just spoken. "Virginians are always annoyed to hear about Paul Revere, who was actually an old man with a tired horse that left Revere to walk home," Virginia said, somewhat acidly, "while Jack Jouett did far more—he saved the lives of Thomas Jefferson and his legislators. Yet, outside of Virginia, few have ever heard of him."

"Perhaps Jouett didn't have as good a press agent as Paul Revere had in Longfellow, as you always say, Virginia," Burr commented. I asked Virginia to sum up the incident that Ingrid had touched on psychically.

"Jack Jouett was a native of Albemarle County and was of French Huguenot origin. His father, Captain John Jouett, owned this tavern."

"We think there is a chance that he also owned the Cuckoo Tavern in Louisa, forty miles from here," Burr interjected.

"Jouett had a son named Jack who stood six feet, four inches and weighed over two hundred pounds. He was an expert rider and one of those citizens who signed the oath of allegiance to the Commonwealth of Virginia in 1779.

"It was June 3, 1781, and the government had fled to Charlottesville from the advancing British troops. Most of Virginia was in British hands, and General Cornwallis very much wanted to capture the leaders of the Revolution, especially Thomas Jefferson, who had authored the Declaration of Independence, and Patrick Henry, whose motto, 'Give me liberty or give me death,' had so much contributed to the success of the Revolution. In charge of two hundred fifty cavalrymen was Sir Banastre Tarleton. His mission was to get to Charlottesville as quickly as possible to capture the leaders of the uprising. Tarleton was determined to cover the seventy miles' distance between Cornwallis' headquarters and Charlottesville in a single twenty-four-hour period, in order to surprise the leaders of the American independence movement.

"In the town of Louisa, forty miles distant from Charlottesville, he and his men stopped into the Cuckoo Tavern for a brief respite. Fate would have it that Jack Jouett was at the tavern at that moment, looking after his father's business. It was a very hot day for June, and the men were thirsty. Despite Tarleton's orders, their tongues loosened, and Jack Jouett was able to overhear their destination. Jack decided to outride them and warn Charlottesville. It was about 10 P.M. when he got on his best horse, determined to take shortcuts and side roads, while the British would have to stick to the main road. Fortunately it was a moonlit night; otherwise he might not have made it in the rugged hill country.

"Meanwhile the British were moving ahead too, and around 11 o'clock they came to a halt on a plantation near Louisa. By 2 A.M. they had resumed their forward march. They paused again a few hours later to seize and burn a train of twelve wagons loaded with arms and clothing for the Continental troops in South Carolina. When dawn broke over Charlottesville, Jouett had left the British far behind. Arriving at Monticello, he dashed up to the front entrance to rouse Jefferson; however, Governor Jefferson, who was an early riser, had seen the rider tear up his driveway and met him at the door. Ever the gentleman, Jefferson offered the exhausted messenger a glass of wine before allowing him to proceed to Charlottesville proper, two miles farther on. There he roused the other members of the government, while Jefferson woke his family. Two hours later, when Tarleton came thundering into Charlottesville, the government of Virginia had vanished."

"That's quite a story, Virginia," I said.

"Of course," Burr added, "Tarleton and his men might have been here even earlier if it hadn't been for the fact that they first stopped at Castle Hill. Dr. and Mrs. Walker entertained them lavishly and served them a sumptuous breakfast. It was not only sumptuous but also delaying, and Dr. Walker played the perfect host to the hilt, showing Tarleton about the place despite the British commander's impatience, even to measuring Tarleton's orderly on the living-room door jamb. This trooper was the tallest man in the British army and proved to be 6' 9¼" tall. Due to these and other delaying tactics—the Walkers made Jack Jouett's ride a complete success. Several members of the legislature who were visiting Dr. Walker at the time were captured, but Jefferson and the bulk of the legislature, which had just begun to convene that morning, got away.

After Thomas Jefferson had taken refuge at the house of Mr. Cole, where he was not likely to be found, Jouett went to his room at his father's tavern, the very house we were in. He had well deserved his rest. Among those who were hiding from British arrest was Patrick Henry. He arrived at a certain farmhouse and identified himself by saying, "I'm Patrick Henry." But the farmer's wife replied, "Oh, you couldn't be, because my husband is out there fighting, and Patrick Henry would be out there too." Henry managed to convince the farmer's wife that his life depended on his hiding in her house, and finally she understood. But it was toward the end of the Revolutionary War and the British knew very well that they had for all intents and purposes been beaten. Consequently, shortly afterward, Cornwallis suggested to the Virginia legislators that they return to Charlottesville to resume their offices.

It was time to proceed to Monticello; the afternoon sun was

setting, and we would be arriving just after the last tourists had left. Monticello, which every child knows from its representation on the American five-cent piece, is probably one of the finest examples of American architecture, designed by Jefferson himself, who lies buried there in the family graveyard. It stands on a hill looking down into the valley of Charlottesville. Carefully landscaped grounds surround the house. Inside, the house is laid out in classical proportions. From the entrance hall with its famous clock, also designed by Jefferson, one enters a large, round room, the heart of the house. On both sides of this central area are rectangular rooms. To the left is a corner room, used as a study and library from where Jefferson, frequently in the morning before anyone else was up, used to look out on the rolling hills of Virginia. Adjacent to it is a very small bedroom, almost a bunk. Thus, the entire west wing of the building is a self-contained apartment in which Jefferson could be active without interfering with the rest of his family. In the other side of the round central room is a large dining room leading to a terrace which, in turn, continues into an open walk with a magnificent view of the hillside. The furniture is Jefferson's own, as are the silver and china, some of it returned to Monticello by history-conscious citizens of the area who had previously purchased it.

The first room we visited was Jefferson's bedroom. Almost in awe herself, Ingrid touched the bedspread of what was once Jefferson's bed, then his desk, and the books he had handled. "I feel his presence here," she said, "and I think he did a lot of his work in this room, a lot of planning and working things out, till the wee hours of the night." I don't think Ingrid knew that Jefferson was in the habit of doing just that, in this particular room.

I motioned Ingrid to sit down in one of Jefferson's chairs and try to capture whatever she might receive from the past. "I can see an awful lot of hard work, sleepless nights, and turmoil. Other than that, nothing."

We went into the library next to the study. "I don't think he spent much time here really, just for reference." On we went to the dining room to the right of the central room. "I think this was his favorite room, and he loved to meet people here socially." Then she added, "I get the words 'plum pudding' and 'hot liquor.'"

"Well," Burr commented, "he loved the lighter things of life. He brought ice cream to America, and he squirted milk directly from the cow into a goblet to make it froth. He had a French palate. He liked what we used to call floating island, a very elaborate dessert."

"I see a lot of people. It is a friendly gathering with glittering glasses and candlelight," Ingrid said. "They are elegant but don't have on overcoats. I see their white silken shirts. I see them laughing and passing things around. Jefferson is at the table with white hair pulled back, leaning over and laughing."

The sun was setting, since it was getting toward half past six now, and we started to walk out the French glass doors onto the terrace. From there an open walk led around a sharp corner to a small building, perhaps twenty or twenty-five yards in the distance. Built in the same classical American style as Monticello itself, the building contained two fair-sized rooms, on two stories. The walk led to the entrance to the upper story, barricaded by an iron grillwork to keep tourists out. It allowed us to enter the room only partially, but sufficiently for Ingrid to get her bearings. Outside, the temperature sank rapidly as the evening approached. A wind had risen, and so it was pleasant to be inside the protective walls of the little house.

"Horace, where are we now?" I asked.

"We are in the honeymoon cottage where Thomas Jefferson brought his bride and lived at the time when his men were building Monticello. Jefferson and his family lived here at the very beginning, so you might say that whatever impressions there are here would be of the pre-Revolutionary part of Jefferson's life."

I turned to Ingrid and asked for her impressions. "I feel everything is very personal here and light, and I don't feel the tremendous strain in the planning of things I felt in the Monticello building. As I close my eyes, I get a funny feeling about a bouquet of flowers, some very strong and peculiar exotic flowers. They are either pink or light red and have a funny name, and I have a feeling that a woman involved in this impression is particularly fond of a specific kind of flower. He goes out of his way to get them for her, and I also get the feeling of a liking for a certain kind of china porcelain. Someone is a collector and wants to buy certain things, being a connoisseur, and wants to have little knick-knacks all over the place. I don't know if any of this makes any sense, but this is how I see it."

"It makes sense indeed," Horace Burr replied. "Jefferson did more to import rare trees and rare flowering shrubs than anyone else around here. In fact, he sent shipments back from France while he stayed there and indicated that they were so rare that if you planted them in one place they might not succeed. So he planted only a third at Monticello, a third at Verdant Lawn, which is an old estate belonging to a friend of his, and a third somewhere else in Virginia. It was his idea to plant them in three places to see if they would thrive in his Virginia."

"The name Rousseau comes to mind. Did he know anyone by that name?" Ingrid asked.

"Of course, he was much influenced by Rousseau."

"I also get the feeling of a flickering flame, a habit of staying up to all hours of the morning. Oh, and is there any historical record of an argument concerning this habit of his, between his wife and himself and some kind of peacemaking gesture on someone else's part?"

"I am sure there was an argument," Horace said, "but I doubt that there ever was a peacemaking gesture. You see, their marriage was not a blissful one; she was very wealthy and he spent her entire estate, just as he spent Dabney Carr's entire estate and George Short's entire estate. He went through estate after estate, including his own. Dabney Carr was his cousin, and he married Jefferson's sister, Martha. He was very wealthy, but Jefferson gathered up his sister and the children and brought them here after Carr's death. He then took over all the plantations and effects of Mr. Carr.

"Jefferson was a collector of things. He wrote three catalogues of his own collection, and when he died it was the largest collection in America. You are right about the porcelain, because it was terribly sophisticated at that time to be up on porcelain. The clipper trade was bringing in these rarities, and he liked to collect them."

Since Ingrid had scored so nicely up to now, I asked her whether she felt any particular emotional event connected with this little house.

"Well, I think the wife was not living on her level, her standard, and she was unhappy. It wasn't what she was used to. It wasn't grand enough. I think she had doubts about him and his plans."

"In what sense?"

"I think she was dubious about what would happen. She was worried that he was getting too involved, and she didn't like his political affiliations too well."

I turned to Horace for comments. To my surprise, Horace asked me to turn off my tape recorder since the information was of a highly confidential nature. However, he pointed out that the material could be found in American Heritage, and that I was free to tell the story in my own words.

Apparently, there had always been a problem between Jefferson and his wife concerning other women. His associations were many and varied. Perhaps the most lasting was with a beautiful young black woman, about the same age as his wife. She was the illegitimate natural child of W. Skelton, a local gentleman, and served as a personal maid to Mrs. Jefferson. Eventually, Jefferson had a number of children by this woman. He even took her to Paris. He would send for her. This went on for a number of years and eventually contributed to the disillusionment of this woman. She died in a little room upstairs, and they took the coffin up there some way, but when they put it together and got her into the coffin, it wouldn't come downstairs. They had to take all the windows out and lower her on a rope. And what was she doing up there in the first place? All this did not contribute to Mrs. Jefferson's happiness. The tragedy is that, after Jefferson's death, two of his mulatto children were sent to New Orleans and sold as prostitutes to pay his debts. There are said to be some descendants of that liaison alive today, but you won't find any of this in American textbooks.

Gossip and legend intermingle in small towns and in the countryside. This is especially true when important historical figures are involved. So it is said that Jefferson did not die a natural death. Allegedly, he committed suicide by cutting his own throat. Toward the end of Jefferson's life, there was a bitter feud between himself and the Lewis family. Accusations and counteraccusations are said to have gone back and forth. Jefferson is said to have had Merriweather Lewis murdered and, prior to that, to have accused Mr. Lewis of a number of strange things that were not true. But none of these legends and rumors can be proved in terms of judicial procedure; when it comes to patriotic heroes of the American Revolution, the line between truth and fiction is always rather indistinct.

3. "SHIP OF DESTINY": THE U. S. F. CONSTELLATION

THE DARK BUICK RACED THROUGH the windy night, turning corners rather more sharply than it should: But the expedition was an hour late, and there were important people awaiting our arrival. It was 9 o'clock in the evening, and at that time Baltimore is pretty tame: Traffic had dwindled down to a mere trickle, and the chilly October weather probably kept many pedestrians indoors, so we managed to cross town at a fast clip.

Jim Lyons had come to pick us up at the hotel minutes before, and the three committee members awaiting us at the waterfront had been there since 8 o'clock. But I had arrived late from Washington, and Sybil Leek had only just joined us: She had come down from New York without the slightest idea why I had summoned her. This was all good sport to my psychic associate, and the dark streets which we now left behind for more open territory meant nothing to her. She knew this was Baltimore, and a moment later she realized we were near water: You couldn't very well mistake the hulls of ships silhouetted against the semidark sky, a sky faintly lit by the reflections from the city's downtown lights.

The car came to a screeching halt at the end of a pier. Despite the warmth of the heater, we were eager to get out into the open.

The excitement of the adventure was upon us.

As we piled out of Jim Lyons' car, we noticed three shivering men standing in front of a large, dark shape. That shape, on close inspection, turned out to be the hull of a large sailing ship. For the moment, however, we exchanged greetings and explained our tardiness: little comfort to men who had been freezing for a full hour! The three committee members were Gordon Stick, chairman of the Constellation restoration committee, Jean Hofmeister, the tall, gaunt harbormaster of Baltimore, and Donald Stewart, the curator of the ancient ship and a professional historian.

Although Sybil realized she was in front of a large ship, she had no idea of what sort of ship it was; only a single, faint bulb inside the hull cast a little light on the scene, and nobody had mentioned anything about the ship or the purpose of our visit.

There was no superstructure visible, and no masts, and suddenly I remembered that Jim Lyons had casually warned me—the old ship was "in repair" and not its true self as yet. How accurate this was I began to realize a moment later when we started to board her. I was looking for the gangplank or stairway to enter.

The harbormaster shook his head with a knowing smile.

"I'm afraid you'll have to rough it, Mr. Holzer," he said.

He then shone his miner's lamp upon the black hull. There was a rope ladder hanging from a plank protruding from the deck. Beyond the plank, there seemed to be a dark, gaping hole, which, he assured me, led directly into the interior of the ship. The trick was not to miss it, of course. If one did, there was a lot of water below. The ship lay about two yards from the pier, enough room to drown, if one were to be so clumsy as to fall off the ladder or miss the plank. I looked at the rope ladder swaying in the cold October wind, felt the heavy tape recorder tugging at my back and the camera around my neck, and said to myself, "Hans, you're going for a bath. How do I get out of all this?"

Now I'm not a coward normally, but I hate taking chances. Right now I wished I were someplace else. Anyplace except on this chilly pier in Baltimore. While I was still wrestling with words to find the right formula that would get me off the hook, I saw Sybil Leek, who is not a small woman, hurry up that rope ladder with the agility of a mother hen rushing home to the coop for supper. In a second, she had disappeared into the hull of the ship. I swallowed hard and painfully and said to myself, if Sybil can do it, so can I. Bravely, I grabbed the ladder and hauled myself up, all the while sending thought messages to my loved ones, just in case I didn't make it. Step by step, farther and farther away from firm ground I went. I didn't dare look back, for if I had I am sure the others would have looked like dwarfs to me by now. Finally I saw the wooden plank sticking out of the hull, and like a pirate-condemned sailor in reverse I walked the plank, head down, tape recorder banging against my ribs, camera hitting my eyeballs, not daring to stand up lest I hit the beams—until I was at the hole; then, going down on my knees, I half crawled into the hull of the ship where I found Sybil whistling to herself, presumably a sailor's tune. At least I had gotten inside. How I would eventually get back out again was a subject too gruesome to consider at that moment. It might well be that I would have to remain on board until a gangplank had been installed, but for the moment at least I was safe and could begin to feel human again. The others had now followed us up the ladder, and everybody was ready to begin the adventure. There was just enough light to make out the ancient beams and wooden companionways, bunks, bulkheads, and what have you: A very old wooden ship lay before us, in the state of total disrepair with its innards torn open and its sides exposed, but still afloat and basically sound and strong. Nothing whatever was labeled or gave away the name of our ship, nor were there any dates or other details as the restoration had not yet begun in earnest and only the outer hull had been secured as a first step. Sybil had no way of knowing anything about the ship, except that which her own common sense told her—a very old wooden ship. For that reason, I had chosen the dark of night for our adventure in Baltimore, and I had pledged the men to keep quiet about everything until we had completed our investigation.

I first heard about this remarkable ship, the frigate Constellation, when Jim Lyons, a TV personality in Baltimore, wrote to me and asked me to have a psychic look at the historic ship. There had been reports of strange happenings aboard, and there were a number of unresolved historical questions involving the ship. Would I come down to see if I could unravel some of those ancient mysteries? The frigate was built in 1797, the first man-of-war of the United States. As late as World War II she was still in commission—something no other ship that old ever accomplished. Whenever Congress passed a bill decommissioning the old relic, something happened to stay its hands: Patriotic committees sprang up and raised funds, or individuals in Washington would suddenly come to the rescue, and the scrappy ship stayed out of the scrapyard. It was as if something, or someone, was at work, refusing to let the ship die. Perhaps some of this mystic influence rubbed off on President Franklin Roosevelt, a man who was interested in psychic research as was his mother, Sarah Delano Roosevelt. At any rate, when the Constellation lay forgotten at Newport, Rhode Island, and the voices demanding her demolition were louder than ever, Roosevelt reacted as if the mysterious power aboard the frigate had somehow reached out to him: In 1940, at the height of World War II, he decreed that the frigate Constellation should be the flagship of the U. S. Atlantic Fleet!

Long after our remarkable visit to Baltimore on a windy October night, I got to know the remarkable ship a lot better. At the time, I did not wish to clutter my unconscious mind with detailed knowledge of her history, so that Sybil Leek could not be accused of having obtained data from it.

The year was 1782. The United States had been victorious in its war for independence, and the new nation could well afford to disband its armed forces. Commerce with foreign countries thrived, and American merchant ships appeared in increasing numbers on the high seas. But a nation then as now is only as strong as her ability to defend herself from enemy attacks. Soon the marauding freebooters of North Africa and the Caribbean made American shipping unsafe, and many sailors fell into pirate hands. Finally, in 1794, Congress decided to do something about this situation, and authorized the construction of six men-of-war or frigates to protect American shipping abroad. The bill was duly signed by George Washington, and work on the ships started immediately. However, only three of these ships, meant to be sister ships, were built in time for immediate action. The first frigate, and thus the very oldest ship in the U. S. Navy, was the U. S. F. Constellation, followed by the Constitution and the United States. The Constellation had three main masts, a wooden hull, and thirty-six guns, while the other two ships had forty-four guns each. But the Constellation's builder, David Stodder of Baltimore, gave her his own patented sharp bow lines, a feature later famous with the Baltimore Clippers. This design gave the ships greater speed, and earned the Constellation, after she had been launched, the nickname of "Yankee Race Horse."

On June 26, 1798, the brand-new frigate put out to sea from Baltimore, then an important American seaport, and headed for the Caribbean. She was under the command of a veteran of the Revolutionary War by the name of Thomas Truxtun, who was known for his efficiency and stern views in matters of discipline. A month after the ship had arrived in the area to guard American shipping, she saw action for the first time. Although the North African menace had been subdued for the time being in the wake of a treaty with the Barbary chieftains, the French menace in the Caribbean was as potent as ever.

Consequently, it was with great eagerness that the crew of the Constellation came upon the famous French frigate L'Insurgente passing near the island of Nevis on a balmy February day in 1799. Within an hour after the first broadside, the French warship was a helpless wreck. This first United States naval victory gave the young nation a sense of dignity and pride which was even more pronounced a year later when the Constellation met up with the French frigate La Vengeance. Although the American ship had increased its guns by two, to a total of thirty-eight, she was still outclassed by the French raider sporting fifty-two guns. The West Indian battle between the two naval giants raged for five hours. Then the French ship, badly battered, escaped into the night.

America was feeling its oats now; although only a handful of countries had established close relations with the new republic, and the recently won freedom from Britain was far from secure,

Congress felt it would rather fight than submit to blackmail and holdup tactics.

Although Captain Truxtun left the Constellation at the end of 1801, his drill manual and tactical methods became the basis for all later U. S. Navy procedures. Next to command the Constellation was Alexander Murray, whose first mission was to sail for the Mediterranean in 1802 to help suppress the Barbary pirates, who had once again started to harass American shipping. During the ensuing blockade of Tripoli, the Constellation saw much action, sinking two Arab ships and eventually returning to her home port in late 1805 after a peace treaty had finally been concluded with the Arab pirates.

For seven years there was peace, and the stately ship lay in port at Washington. Then in 1812, when war with Britain erupted again, she was sent to Hampton Roads, Virginia, to help defend the American installations at Fort Craney. But as soon as peace returned between the erstwhile colonies and the former motherland, the Barbary pirates acted up again, and it was deemed necessary to go to war against them once more.

This time the Constellation was part of Stephen Decatur's squadron, and remained in North African waters until 1817 to enforce the new peace treaty with Algeria.

America was on the move, expanding not only overland and winning its own West, but opening up new trade routes overseas. Keeping pace with its expanding merchant fleet was a strong, if small, naval arm. Again, the Constellation guarded American shipping off South America between 1819 and 1821, then sailed around the Cape to the Pacific side of the continent, and finally put down the last Caribbean pirates in 1826. Later she was involved in the suppression of the Seminole Indian rebellion in Florida, and served as Admiral Dallas's flagship. In 1840 she was sent on a wide-ranging trip, sailing from Boston to Rio de Janeiro under the command of Commodore Lawrence Kearny. From there she crossed the Pacific Ocean to open up China for American trade; returning home via Hawaii, Kearny was able, in the proverbial nick of time, to prevent a British plot to seize the islands.

The British warship H. M. S. Caryfoot had been at anchor at Honolulu when the Constellation showed up. Hastily, the British disavowed a pledge by King Kamehameha III to turn over the reins of government to the ship's captain, and native rule was restored. For a few years, the famous old ship rested in its berth at Norfolk, Virginia. She had deserved her temporary retirement, having logged some 58,000 miles on her last trip alone, all of it with sail power only. In 1853 it was decided to give her an overhaul. After all, the Navy's oldest ship was now fifty-five years old and showed some stress and strain. The rebuilding included the addition of twelve feet to her length, and her reclassification as a twenty-two-gun sloop of war. Most of her original timber was kept, repairing and replacing only what was worn out. Once more the veteran ship sailed for the Mediterranean, but the handwriting was already on the wall: In 1858, she was decommissioned.

Here the mysterious force that refused to let the ship die came into play again.

When civil war seemed inevitable between North and South, the Constellation was brought back into service in 1859 to become the flagship of the African squadron. Her job was intercepting slave ships bound for the United States, and she managed to return a thousand slaves to their native Africa.

Outbreak of war brought her back home in 1861, and after another stint in the Mediterranean protecting United States shipping from marauding Confederate raiders, she became a receiving and training ship at Hampton Roads, Virginia.

Sailing ships had seen their day, and the inevitable seemed at hand: Like so many wooden sailing ships, she would eventually be destined for the scrapheap. But again she was saved from this fate. The Navy returned her to active service in 1871 as a training ship at the Annapolis Naval Academy. The training period was occasionally interrupted by further sea missions, such as her errand of mercy to Ireland during the 1880 famine. Gradually, the old ship had become a symbol of American naval tradition and was known the world over. In 1894, almost a hundred years old now, the still-seaworthy man-of-war returned to Newport for another training mission. By 1914, her home port Baltimore claimed the veteran for a centennial celebration, and she would have continued her glorious career as an active seagoing ship of the U. S. Navy, forever, had it not been for World War II. More important matters took precedence over the welfare of the Constellation, which lay forgotten at the Newport berth. Gradually, her condition worsened, and ultimately she was no longer capable of putting out to sea.

When the plight of this ancient sailor was brought to President Roosevelt's attention, he honored her by making her once again the flagship of the U. S. Atlantic Fleet. But the honor was not followed by funds to restore her to her erstwhile glory. After the war she was berthed in Boston, where attempts were made to raise funds by allowing visitors aboard. By 1953, the ship was in such poor condition that her total loss seemed only a matter of time.

At this moment, a committee of patriotic Baltimore citizens decided to pick up the challenge. As a first step, the group secured title to the relic from the U. S. Navy. Next, the ship was brought home to Baltimore, like a senior citizen finally led back to its native habitat. All the tender care of a sentimental association was lavished on her, and with the help of volunteers, the restoration committee managed to raise the necessary funds to restore the Constellation to its original appearance, inside and out. At the time of our nocturnal visit, only the first stage of the restoration had been undertaken: to make her hull seaworthy so she could safely stay afloat at her berth. In the summer of 1968, the rest of the work would be undertaken, but at the time of our visit, the inside was still a raw assortment of wooden beams and badly hinged doors, her superstructure reduced to a mastless flat deck and the original corridors and companionways in their grime-covered state. All this would eventually give way to a spick-and-span ship, as much the pride of America in 1968 as she was back in 1797 when she was launched. But apart from the strange way in which fate seemed to prevent the destruction of this proud sailing ship time and again, other events had given the Constellation the reputation of a haunted ship. This fame was not especially welcomed by the restoration committee, of course, and it was never encouraged, but for the sake of the record, they did admit and document certain strange happenings aboard the ship. In Donald Stewart, the committee had the services of a trained historian, and they hastened to make him the curator of their floating museum.

Whether or not any psychic occurrences took place aboard the Constellation prior to her acquisition by the committee is not known, but shortly after the Baltimore group had brought her into Baltimore drydock, a strange incident took place. On July 26, 1959, a Roman Catholic priest boarded the ship, which was then already open to the public, although not in very good condition.

The priest had read about the famous ship, and asked curator Donald Stewart if he might come aboard even though it was before the 10 A.M. opening hour for visitors. He had to catch a train for Washington at eleven, and would never be able to face his flock back in Detroit without having seen so famed a vessel. The curator gladly waived the rules, and the good father ascended. However, since Mr. Stewart was in the midst of taking inventory and could not spare the time to show him around, he suggested that the priest just walk around on his own.

At 10:25, the priest returned from below deck, looking very cheerful. Again the curator apologized for not having taken him around.

"That's all right," the man of the cloth replied, "the old gent showed me around."

"What old gent?" the curator demanded. "There is nobody else aboard except you and me."

The priest protested. He had been met by an old man in a naval uniform, he explained, and the fellow had shown him around below. The man knew his ship well, for he was able to point out some of the gear and battle stations.

"Ridiculous," bellowed Mr. Stewart, who is a very practical Scotsman. "Let's have a look below."

Both men descended into the hull and searched the ship from bow to stern. Not a living soul was to be found outside of their own good selves.

When they returned topside, the priest was no longer smiling. Instead, he hurriedly left, pale and shaken, to catch that train to Washington. He knew he had met an old sailor, and he knew he was cold sober when he did.

Donald Stewart's curiosity, however, was aroused, and he looked into the background of the ship a bit more closely. He discovered then that similar experiences had happened to naval personnel when the ship was at Newport, Rhode Island, and to watchmen aboard the Constellation. Nobody liked to talk about them, however. On one occasion during the summer a figure was seen aboard on the gun deck after the ship had closed for the day and no visitors could be aboard. The police were called to rout the burglar or intruder and they brought with them a police dog, a fierce-looking German shepherd, who was immediately sent below deck to rout the intruder. But instead of following orders as he always did, the dog stood frozen to the spot, shivering with fear, hair on his neck bristling, and refused to budge or go below. It is needless to point out that no human intruder was found on that occasion.

Another time a group of Sea Scouts was holding a meeting aboard. The idea was to give the proceedings a real nautical flavor. The fact that the ship was tied up solidly and could not move did not take away from the atmosphere of being aboard a real seagoing vessel. Suddenly, as if moved by unseen hands, the wheel spun from port to starboard rapidly. Everyone in the group saw it, and pandemonium broke loose. There wasn't any wind to account for a movement of the ship. Furthermore, the spool of the wheel was not even linked to the rudder!

The Constellation had returned to Baltimore in August 1955. While still under Navy jurisdiction, the first of the unusual incidents took place. The vessel was then tied up beside the U. S. S. Pike at the Naval Training Center. There was never anyone aboard at night. The dock was well guarded, and strangers could not approach without being challenged. Nevertheless, a Navy commander and his men reported that they had seen "someone in an early uniform" walking the quarterdeck at night. The matter was investigated by the Baltimore Sun, which also published the testimonies of the Navy personnel. When the newspaper sent a photographer aboard the Constellation, however, every one of his photographs was immediately seized by naval authorities without further explanation.

Jim Lyons, a longtime Baltimore resident, was able to add another detail to the later uncanny events recorded by the curator. During a Halloween meeting of the Sea Scouts, which was followed by a dance, one of the girls present had an unusual experience. Seated on a wall bench, she turned to speak to what she thought was her escort, and instead looked directly into the face of an old sailor, who smiled at her and then disappeared! Since she had never heard of any alleged hauntings aboard ship, her mind was not impressed with any such suggestion. She described the apparition exactly as the priest had described his ghostly guide below deck. Very likely other visitors to the ship may have had strange encounters of this sort without reporting them, since people tend to disregard or suppress that which does not easily fall into categories they can accept.

It was clear from these reports that some restless force was still active aboard the old vessel, and that it wanted the Constellation to go on unharmed and as she was in her heyday. But why did the ghostly sailor make such an effort to manifest and to cling to this ship? What was the secret that this "ship of destiny" harbored below deck?

We were standing in a small group on the main deck of the ship when Sybil said hurriedly, "Must go down below," and before we could even ask her why, she had descended the narrow ladder leading to the next lower level. There she deftly made for the after orlop deck, where she stopped abruptly and remarked, "There is much evil here!"

Before we had all come aboard, she had been wandering about the ship in almost total darkness. "I personally have been with the ship for eleven years," the curator later observed, "and I would not attempt such a feat without light, although I know the ship like the back of my hand." Earlier, while we were still en route to the harbor, Sybil had suddenly mumbled a date out of context and apparently for no particular reason. That date was 1802. When I had questioned her about it she only said it had significance for the place we were going to visit. Later I discovered that the first captain of the Constellation had left the frigate at the end of 1801, and that 1802 signified a new and important chapter in the ship's career.

How could Sybil deduce this from the modern streets of nocturnal Baltimore through which we had been driving at the time? And now we were finally aboard, waiting for developments. These were not long in coming. As Sybil went down into the hold of the ship, we followed her. As if she knew where she was going, she directed her steps toward the ladder area of the after orlop deck.

"I'm frightened," she said, and shuddered. For a person like Sybil to be frightened was most unusual. She showed me her arms, which were covered with gooseflesh. It was not particularly cold inside the hold, and none of us showed any such symptoms.

"This area has a presence, lots of atmosphere…very cruel. And I heard what sounded like a baby crying. Why would a baby cry aboard a ship like this?"

Why indeed?

"A peculiar death…a boy…a gun…big gun…a bad deed…."

"Is this boy connected with the ship?"

Instead of answering, she seemed to take in the atmosphere. More and more dissociating herself from us and the present, she mumbled, "Seventeen sixty-five."

The date had no significance for the ship, but probably for its first captain, then still in British service.

"French guns...."

This would refer to the two great engagements with the French fleet in 1799 and 1800.

I tried to get back to the boy.

"He walked around this boat a lot," Sybil said. "Something happened to him. Have to find the gun. Doesn't like guns. He's frightened. Killed here. Two men...frightening the boy. Powder...powder boy. Eleven."

"Who were those two men?"

"Seventy-two...sixty-six...their boat is not here...."

"Is there an entity present on this boat now?"

"Three people. Boy and the two men."

"Who are the two men?"

Belabored, breathing heavily, Sybil answered.

"Thraxton...captain...Thomas...T-h-r...I can't get the middle of it...1802...other man...to the gun...."

When these words came from Sybil's now half-entranced lips, the little group around me froze. I heard a gasp from one of them and realized that Sybil must have hit on something important. Only later did I learn that Captain Thomas Truxtun was the ship's first captain, and that he had been replaced by another at the beginning of 1802. If he was one of the ghostly presences here, he certainly had a reason to stay with the ship that he had made great and whose name was forever linked with his own in naval history.

Sybil came out of her semi-trance momentarily and complained she wasn't getting through too well. "Name ending in son," she said now. "Harson...can't hear it too well. I hear a lot of noise from guns. Attacking. Seventy-two. Sixty-four. French. I can't see what happened to the boy. He didn't come back. But he's here now. It's confusing me. Fire!"

"Can you get more about the two men with the boy?" I asked.

"One is important, the other one is...a...armory...the guns...tends to the guns...he's still here...has to be forgiven...for his adventures...he was a coward...he hid away...he was killed by the men on this boat, not the enemy...blew him up...his friends did it because he was a coward...in action...."

"What was his name?"

"Harson...Larson...I don't know....He was an armorer...."

"Where was he from?"

"Sweden."

At this point, when we were leaning over to catch every word of Sybil's testimony, my tape recorder went out of order. No matter how I shook it, it would not work again. Quickly, I tore out a sheet of paper and took notes, later comparing them with those of the curator, Don Stewart.

As I pressed my psychic friend—and her communicators—for more information, she obliged in halting, labored sentences.

This man had been done an injustice, she explained, for he was not a coward. Captain Thomas "Thr-ton," an American, had given the order and he was killed by being blown to bits through a cannon. Finally, the seventy-two sixty-six figures she had mentioned earlier fell into place. That was the spot where the killing happened, she explained, at sea. The position, in other words.

"The guns are a bad influence," she mumbled, "if you take the third gun away it would be better…bad influence here, frightens people…third gun. This ship would be with another… Const… ation, and Con…federation…something like that…should be at sea…not a sister ship but of the same type with a similar spelling of the name, even though this ship was slightly older, they belong together!"

This of course was perfectly true, but she could not have known it from standing in an almost dark hull. The Constellation preceded the Constitution by a very short time.

"1795 important to this boat."

That was the year work on her had begun.

Gradually, I was able to sort out the various tenants of the ship's netherworld.

The eleven-year-old boy was somehow tied to the date of August 16, 1822. He was, Mrs. Leek stated, the victim of murder by two crew members in the cockpit of the orlop deck. Mr. Stewart later confirmed that very young boys were used aboard old ships to serve as lolly boys or servants to naval surgeons. The area where the ghostly boy was most active, according to the psychic, was precisely what had been the surgeon's quarters!

The man who had been executed as a coward during action against the French, as the medium had said, could not materialize because he was in bits and pieces and thus remembered "himself" in this gruesome fashion.

The man who had condemned him was Captain Thomas Truxtun, and the man's name was something like Harsen. But here confusion set in. For she also felt the influence of a person named Larsen—a Swede, she thought—and he gave two figures similar to the other figures mentioned before, 73 and 66, and we'd know him by those numerals!

It now became clear to me that Mrs. Leek was getting impressions from several layers at the same time and that I would have to separate them to come to any kind of rational evaluation of the material.

I brought her out of her semi-trance state and we started to discuss what had come through her, when all of a sudden the large doors at the bottom of the ladder approximately ten feet away slowly opened by themselves. The curator, who saw this, reports that a rush of cold air followed. He had often noticed that there was a temperature differential of some five degrees between the after crew's ladder area and the rest of the ship, for which there was no satisfactory explanation.

It was 10 o'clock when we left the ship, and one by one we descended the perilous ladder. It wasn't easy for me until I left my equipment behind for the moment and bravely grabbed the rope ladder in the dark. The fact that I am writing this account is proof I did not plunge into chilly Baltimore Harbor, but I wouldn't want to try it again for all the ghosts in America!

We repaired to a harbor tavern, and I started to question Mr. Stewart about the information received through Mrs. Leek. It was there that I first learned about Captain Truxtun, and his connection with the ship. It should be noted that only I was in close proximity of Mrs. Leek during most of the séance—the others kept a certain distance. Thus, any "reading of the minds" of the others who knew this name is not likely, and I did not as yet have this knowledge in my own mind.

But there was more, much more. It would appear that a man was indeed executed for cowardice during the action against the French in 1799, just as Mrs. Leek had said. It was during the battle with L'Insurgente. A sailor named Neil Harvey deserted his position at gun number 7 on the portside. Found by a Lieutenant Starrett, the traditional account has it, he was instantly run through by the officer.

Had Sybil's "Harsen" anything to do with Harvey?

She had stated the gun was number 3, not 7, but on checking it was found that the gun position numbers had been changed later—after the killing—at the time the ship was rebuilt, so that what is today gun 7 was actually gun 3 in 1799!

It was customary in the British (and early American) navies to execute traitors by strapping them to the mouths of cannon and blowing them to bits. If Lieutenant Starrett, in hot anger, had run the sailor through—and we don't know if he was dead from it—it may well be that the captain, when apprised of the event, had ordered the man, wounded or already dead, subjected to what was considered a highly dishonorable death: no body, no burial at sea. These bits of information were found by the curator, Mr. Stewart, in the original ship's log preserved at the Navy Department in Washington.

Apparently, Neil Harvey's job was that of a night watchman as well as gunner. This may have given rise to another version of the tradition, researched for me by Jim Lyons. In this version, Harvey was found fast asleep when he should have stood watch, and, discovered by Captain Truxtun himself, was cursed by his master forever to walk the decks of his ship, after which the captain himself ran him through with his sword.

The records, however, report the killing by Lieutenant Starrett and even speak of the court-martial proceedings against the sailor. He was condemned, according to the log, for deserting his position and was executed aboard by being shot. This would bear out my suggestion that the sword of Lieutenant Starrett did not finish the unfortunate man off altogether.

I had now accounted for the boy, the captain, and the unhappy sailor named Neil Harvey, blown to bits by the gun. But there was still an unresolved portion to the puzzle: the "Swede" Sybil felt present. By no stretch of the imagination could Neil Harvey be called a Scandinavian. Also, the man, she felt, had "spent the happiest days of his life aboard ship as an employee."

One can hardly call an eighteenth-century sailor an employee, and Harvey did not spend any happy days aboard; certainly, at least, this would not be his memory at the time of sudden death.

But the curator informed me that another watchman, curiously enough, had seen Harvey's ghost, or what looked like an old sailor, while playing cards aboard ship. He looked up from his game, casually, and saw the transparent figure going through the wall in front of him. He quit his position in 1963, when an electric burglary alarm system was installed aboard. Originally a Royal Navy cook, the man had come from Denmark—not Sweden—and his name was Carl Hansen. It occurred to me then that Sybil had been confused by two different entities—a Harvey and a Hansen, both of them watchmen, albeit of different periods.

After Hansen retired from his job aboard the Constellation, he evidently was very lonely for his old home—he had lived aboard from 1958 to 1963. He had written hundreds of letters to the Constellation restoration committee begging them to let him have his old position back, even though he had planned to retire to a farm. It was not possible to give him back his job, but the old man visited the ship on many occasions, keeping up a strong emotional tie with it. He died in 1966 at age seventy-three.

Here again one of those strange similarities had confused Sybil. On one occasion she had mentioned the figures seventy-two and sixty-six as applying to a position at sea, while later saying that the man from Sweden could be recognized by the numerals 73 and 66. It struck the curator that he was giving his age and death year in order to be identified properly!

Who then, among these influences aboard, was responsible for the continued resurgence of the old ship? Who wanted her to stay afloat forever, if possible?

Not the eleven-year-old boy, to whom the ship had meant only horror and death.

But perhaps the other three had found at last, something in common: their love for the U. S. F. Constellation.

Captain Truxtun certainly would feel himself bound to his old ship, the ship that shared his glories.

Neil Harvey might have wished to find justice and to clear his name. So long as the ship existed, there was a chance that the records would bear him out.

And lastly, the twentieth-century watchman Hansen, inexorably mixed up with the ship's destiny by his love for her and his lack of any other real focal point, might just have "gotten stuck" there upon death.

The only thing I can say with reasonable certainty is that the Constellation is not likely to disappear from the sea, whether out in the open ocean or safely nestled at her Baltimore dock. She's got three good men to look after her now.

4. THE HAUNTED ROCKING CHAIR AT ASH LAWN

NOT ONLY HOUSES ARE HAUNTED, even furniture can be the recipient of ghostly attention. Not very far from Castle Hill, Virginia is one of America's most important historical buildings, the country home once owned by James Monroe, where he and Thomas Jefferson often exchanged conversation and also may have made some very big political decisions in their time. Today this is a modest appearing cottage, rather than a big manor house, and it is well kept. It may be visited by tourists at certain hours, since it is considered an historical shrine. If any of my readers are in the area and feel like visiting Ash Lawn, I would suggest they do not mention ghosts too openly with the guides or caretakers.

This house, though small and cozy, nevertheless was James Monroe's favorite house even after he moved to the bigger place which became his stately home later on in his career. At Ash Lawn he could get away from his affairs of state, away from public attention, to discuss matters of great concern with his friend Thomas Jefferson who lived only two miles away at Monticello.

Actually the ghostly goings-on center around a certain wooden rocking chair in the main room. This has been seen to rock without benefit of human hands. I don't know how many people have actually seen the chair rock, but Mrs. J. Massey, who lived in the area for many years, has said to me when I visited the place, "I will tell anyone and I have no objection to its being known, that I've seen not once but time and time again the rocking chair rocking exactly as though someone were in it. My brother John has seen it too. Whenever we touched it it would stop rocking."

Who is the ghost in the rocking chair? Perhaps it is only a spirit, not an earthbound ghost, a spirit who has become so attached to his former home and refuge from the affairs of state, that he still likes to sit now and then in his own rocking chair thinking things over.

5. MRS. SURRATT'S GHOST AT FORT MCNAIR

FORT MCNAIR IS ONE of the oldest military posts in the United States and has had many other names. First it was known as the Arsenal, then called the Washington Arsenal, and in 1826 a penitentiary was built on its grounds, which was a grim place indeed. Because of disease, President Lincoln ordered the penitentiary closed in 1862, but as soon as Lincoln had been murdered, the penitentiary was back in business again.

Among the conspirators accused of having murdered President Lincoln, the one innocent person was Mrs. Mary Surratt, whose sole crime consisted of having run a boarding house where her son had met with some of the conspirators. But as I have shown in a separate investigation of the boarding house in Clifton, Maryland, her son John Surratt was actually a double-agent, so the irony is even greater. She was the first woman hanged in the United States, and today historians are fully convinced that she was totally innocent. The trial itself was conducted in a most undemocratic manner, and it is clear in retrospect that the conspirators never had a chance. But the real power behind the Lincoln assassination, who might have been one of his own political associates, wanted to make sure no one was left who knew anything about the plot, and so Mary Surratt had to be sacrificed.

There is a small, ordinary looking building called Building 21 at Fort McNair, not far from what is now a pleasant tennis court. It was in this building that Mary Surratt was imprisoned and to this day sobs are being heard in the early hours of the morning by a number of people being quartered in the building. The penitentiary stands no more and the land itself is now part of the tennis court. Next to Building 21 is an even smaller house, which serves as quarters for a number of officers. When I visited the post a few years ago, the Deputy Post Commander was quartered there. Building 20 contains five apartments, which have been remodeled a few years ago. The ceilings have been lowered, the original wooden floors have been replaced with asbestos tile. Unexplained fires occurred there in the 1960s. The execution of the conspirators, including Mrs. Mary Surratt, took place just a few yards from where Building 21 now stands. The graves of the hanged conspirators were in what is now the tennis court, but the coffins were removed a few years after the trial and there are no longer any bodies in the ground.

Captain X.—and his name must remain secret for obvious reasons—had lived in apartment number 5 for several years prior to my interviewing him. He has not heard the sobbing of Mary Surratt but he has heard a strange sound, like high wind.

However, Captain and Mrs. C. occupied quarters on the third floor of Building 20 for several years until 1972. This building, incidentally, is the only part of the former penitentiary still standing. The C.s' apartment consisted of the entire third floor and it was on this floor that the conspirators, including John Wilkes Booth, who was already dead, were tried and sentenced to die by hanging. Mary Surratt's cell was also located on the third floor of the building. Mrs. C. has had ESP experiences before, but she was not quite prepared for what occurred to her when she moved onto the post at Fort McNair.

"My experiences in our apartment at Fort McNair were quite unlike any other I have ever known.

"On several occasions, very late at night, someone could be heard walking above, yet we were on the top floor." One night the walking became quite heavy, and a window in the room which had been Mrs. Surratt's cell was continually being rattled, as if someone were trying to get in or out, and there seemed to be a definite presence in the house. This happened in April, as did the trial of the conspirators.

I doubt that it would be easy to visit Fort McNair for any except official reasons, such as perhaps an historical investigation. But for better or for worse the building in question is located on the northeast corner of the tennis courts and Fort McNair itself is in Washington, D.C., at the corner of Fourth and P Streets and easy to reach from the center of the city.

6. A GHOST'S LAST REFUGE

NEAR CHARLOTTESVILLE, VIRGINIA, stands a farmhouse built during Revolutionary days, now owned by Mary W., a lady in her early fifties, who, some years ago, had a fleeting interest in the work of Professor Rhine at Duke University.

Her own psychic talents are acknowledged, but she insists she has not done any automatic writing lately and isn't really very much interested anymore. Later I realized that her waning interest must have some connection with the events at the house which we shall call Wickham, since the real name must at present remain veiled in deference to the owner's request.

Virginia Cloud had come along to serve as a combination guide and clairvoyant, and writer Booton Herndon also came along to observe what he had always found a fascinating subject. Thus a caravan of two cars made its way to Wickham one bright May morning when nature's brilliance belied the sober subject of our goal.

On arrival, my wife, Catherine, and I sat down with Mary W. to hear her tell of her own experiences in the haunted house. Only after she had done so did Virginia Cloud enter the house.

The oldest part of the house, rather skilfully connected to the rest, consists of a hall or main room and a small bedroom reached by a narrow winding staircase.

This portion, dating back to 1781, has been the location of some uncanny happenings beginning at the time when Mrs. W. acquired the house and acreage in 1951. Whether previous owners had had any experiences couldn't be ascertained.

Emotionally keyed at the time, Mrs. W. recalls, she was in a small adjoining room downstairs, which has been turned into a small home bar, when she clearly heard footsteps in the main room, and a noise like that made by riding clothes, swishing sounds; she called out, but she knew it was not her husband; the steps continued; someone was walking up and down in the room. Mrs. W. took a look through the window and saw her entire family outside near the barn, some twenty yards away.

This alarmed her even more and she stepped into the main room. There was no one there. But the eerie thing was that even in her presence the steps continued, reached the doorway and then went back across the room to the stairway where they stopped abruptly at the landing leading to old room above.

The previous owner, by the name of Deauwell, had told Mary W. that when his predecessor at the house, Mrs. Early, had died, there had been a strange noise as if someone were falling down stairs.

Two years later, in 1953, Mrs. W.'s two girls, aged twelve and nine at the time, were playing in the upstairs room while the parents were entertaining some guests in the nearby cottage apart from the main house. It was 10 P.M. when the girls distinctly heard someone walk around downstairs in the empty house. They called out, but got no answer. They thought it was a friend of their parents, but later checking revealed nobody had left the party to return to the main house even for a moment.

Around 1960–61, Mrs. W. again heard the by-now-familiar foot-steps in the same spot. They started, then stopped, then started up again. Although Mrs. W. admitted some psychic talent, her automatic writing had yielded no one claiming to be connected with the house except perhaps a slave girl named Rebecca, who claimed to have been captured by Indians who cut out her tongue; she was found by the Early sons, and became their servant since; Mrs. W. also claimed a guide or control named Robert.

The place had been in litigation for many years, and there are no less than three family cemeteries on the grounds. The house itself was built by one Richard Durrette in 1781. When the fireplace was rebuilt prior to 1938, before Mrs. W. owned the place, an inscription turned up explaining that Hessian-soldier prisoners from a nearby barracks had helped build the chimney in 1781. Three thousand prisoners were kept in barracks nearby. Some stayed afterwards and married local girls.

This was not discussed in the presence of Virginia Cloud, who soon went into semi-trance in the presence of Mary W. and myself. She "saw" an Albert or Alfred, in a white shirt, boots, trousers, but not a uniform, dragging himself into the house; perhaps he was an injured Hessian entering an empty house, chased here by Redcoats. "The British are farther away…. Something was burned near here." At this point, both Mary W. and I smelled smoke. Independent of Virginia Cloud's testimony, both of us also heard a faint knock at the entrance door, two short raps.

Virginia, in her chair near the stairway, started to shiver. "The ghost remembers his mother and calls her, but she is not here any more…only a memory; he may have died here, since I don't see him leave again. His arm is hurt by metal, perhaps a shell."

Mary W. had lived through tragedy in her own life. Her husband, Kenneth, had committed suicide in the very house we were visiting. I had the feeling that Mary's interest in the occult coincided with this event, and that perhaps she thought the ghostly footsteps were actually her late husband's restless movements in the room he had called his own.

But the noises and disturbances go back farther than Mary's tenancy of the house. Premeditated suicide seldom yields ghosts. I am convinced that the ghost at Wickham is not Mary's husband, but the Hessian deserter who wanted to find refuge from the pursuing British.

7. THE OCTAGON GHOSTS

COLONEL JOHN TAYLOE, in 1800, built his mansion, the magnificent building now known as the Octagon because of its shape. It stood in a fashionable part of Washington, but now houses the offices and exhibit of the American Institute of Architects.
In the early 1800s the Colonel's daughter ran away with a stranger and later returned home, asking forgiveness. This she did not get from her stern father and in despair she threw herself from the third-floor landing of the winding staircase that still graces the mansion. She landed on a spot near the base of the stairs, and this started a series of eerie events recorded in the mansion over the years.

Life magazine reported in an article in 1962 on haunted mansions that some visitors claim to have seen a shadow on the spot where the girl fell, while others refuse to cross the spot for reasons unknown; still others have heard the shriek of the falling girl.

The July, 1959, issue of the *American Institute of Architects' Journal* contains a brief account of the long service record of employee James Cypress. Although he himself never saw any ghosts, he reports that at one time when his wife was ill, the doctor saw a man dressed in the clothes of one hundred fifty years ago coming down the spiral staircase. As the doctor looked at the strange man in puzzlement, the man just disappeared into thin air.

After some correspondence with J. W. Rankin, Director of the Institute, my wife and I finally started out for Washington on May 17, 1963. It was a warm day and the beautiful Georgian mansion, set back from one of the capital's busier streets, promised an adventure into a more relaxed past.

Mr. Rankin received us with interest and showed us around the house which was at that time fortunately empty of tourists and other visitors. It was he who supplied some of the background information on the Octagon, from which I quote:

> The White House and the Octagon are relations, in a way. Both date from the beginning of government in the national capital; the White House was started first but the Octagon was first completed. Both have served as the official residence of the President.
>
> It was early in 1797 that Colonel John Tayloe of Mount Airy, Virginia, felt the need for a town house. Mount Airy was a magnificent plantation of some three thousand acres, on which the Colonel, among many activities, bred and raced horses, but the call of the city was beginning to be felt, even in that early day; Philadelphia was the Colonel's choice, but his friend General Washington painted a glowing picture of what the new national capital might become and persuaded him to build the Octagon in surroundings that were then far removed from urbanity.
>
> On April 19, 1797, Colonel Tayloe purchased for $1,000 from Gustavus W. Scott—one of the original purchasers from the Government on November 21, 1796—Lot 8 in Square 170 in the new plot of Washington. Although, as the sketch of 1813 shows, the site was apparently out in a lonely countryside, the city streets had been definitely plotted, and the corner of New

York Avenue and Eighteenth Street was then where it is today.

Obviously, from a glance at the plot plan, Colonel Tayloe's house derived its unique shape from the angle formed at the junction of these two streets. In spite of the name by which the mansion has always been known, Dr. Thornton could have had no intention of making the plan octagonal; the house planned itself from the street frontages.

Work on the building started in 1798 and progressed under the occasional inspection of General Washington, who did not live to see its completion in 1800. The mansion immediately took its place as a center of official and unofficial social activities. Through its hospitable front door passed Madison, Jefferson, Monroe, Adams, Jackson, Decatur, Porter, Webster, Clay, Lafayette, Von Steuben, Calhoun, Randolph, Van Renssalaer and their ladies.

Social activities were forgotten, however, when the War of 1812 threatened and finally engulfed the new nation's capital. On August 24, 1814, the British left the White House a fire-gutted ruin. Mrs. Tayloe's foresight in establishing the French Minister—with his country's flag—as a house guest may have saved the Octagon from a like fate.

Colonel Tayloe is said to have dispatched a courier from Mount Airy, offering President Madison the use of the mansion, and the Madisons moved in on September 8, 1814.

For more than a year Dolly Madison reigned as hostess of the Octagon. In the tower room just over the entrance President Madison established his study, and here signed the Treaty of Ghent on February 17, 1815, establishing a peace with Great Britain which endures to this day.

After the death of Mrs. John Tayloe in 1855, the Octagon no longer served as the family's town house. That part of Washington lost for a time its residential character and the grand old mansion began to deteriorate.

In 1865 it was used as a school for girls. From 1866 to 1879 the Government rented it for the use of the Hydrographic

Office. As an office and later as a studio dwelling, the Octagon served until about 1885, when it was entrusted by the Tayloe heirs to a caretaker.

Glenn Brown, longtime secretary of the American Institute of Architects, suggested in 1889 that the house would make an appropriate headquarters for the Institute.

When the architects started to rehabilitate the building, it was occupied by ten Negro families. The fine old drawing room was found to be piled four feet deep with rubbish. The whole interior was covered with grime, the fireplaces closed up, windows broken, but the structure, built a century before, had been denied no effort or expense to make it worthy of the Tayloes, and it still stood staunch and sound against time and neglect.

Miraculously the slender balusters of the famous stairway continued to serve, undoubtedly helped by the fact that every fifth baluster is of iron, firmly jointed to the handrail and carriage. Even the Coade Stone mantels in drawing room and dining room, with their deeply undercut sculpture, show not a chip nor scar. They had been brought from London in 1799 and bear that date with the maker's name.

On January 1, 1899, the Institute took formal possession of the rehabilitated mansion, its stable, smokehouse and garden.

So much for the house itself. I was given free rein to interview the staff, and proceeded to do so. I carefully tabulated the testimony given me by the employees individually, and checked the records of each of them for reliability and possible dark spots. There were none.

In view of the fact that nobody was exactly eager to be put down as having heard or seen ghosts, far from seeking publicity or public attention, I can only regard these accounts as respectable experiences of well-balanced individuals.

The building itself was then and still is in the care of Alric H. Clay, a man in his thirties, who is an executive with the title of superintendent. The museum part of the Octagon, different from the large complex of offices of the American Institute of Architects, is under the supervision of Mrs. Belma May, who is its curator. She is assisted by a staff of porters and maids, since on occasion formal dinners or parties take place in the oldest part of the Octagon.

Mrs. May is not given to hallucinations or ghost stories, and in a matter-of-fact voice reported to me what she had experienced in the building. Most of her accounts are of very recent date.

Mrs. May saw the big chandelier swing of its own volition while all windows in the foyer were tightly shut; she mentioned the strange occurrence to a fellow worker. She also hears strange noises, not accounted for, and mostly on Saturdays. On one occasion, Mrs. May, accompanied by porters Allen and Bradley, found tracks of human feet in the otherwise undisturbed dust on the top floor, which had long been closed to the public. The tracks looked to her as "if someone were standing on toes, tiptoeing across the floor." It was from there that the daughter of Colonel Tayloe had jumped.

Mrs. May often smells cooking in the building when there is no party. She also feels "chills" on the first-floor landing.

Caretaker Mathew reports that when he walks up the stairs, he often feels as if someone is walking behind him, especially on the second floor. This is still happening to him now.

Ethel Wilson, who helps with parties, reports "chills" in the cloakroom.

Porter Allen was setting up for a meeting on the ground floor in the spring of 1962, when he heard noises "like someone dragging heavy furniture across the floor upstairs." In March, 1963, he and his colleague saw the steps "move as if someone was walking on them, but there was no one there." This happened at 9:30 A.M.

Porter Bradley has heard groaning, but the sound is hard to pin down as to direction. Several times he has also heard footsteps.

Alric H. Clay was driving by with his wife and two children one evening in the spring of 1962, when he noticed that the lights in the building were on. Leaving his family in the car, he entered the closed building by the back door and found everything locked as it should be. However, in addition to the lights being on, he also noticed that the carpet edge was flipped up at the spot where the girl had fallen to her death in the 1800s.

Clay, not believing in ghosts, went upstairs; there was nobody around, so he turned the lights off put the carpet back as it should be, and went downstairs into the basement where the light controls are.

At that moment, on the main floor above (which he had just left) he clearly heard someone walk from the drawing room to the door and back. Since he had just checked all doors and knew them to be bolted firmly, he was so upset he almost electrocuted himself at the switches. The steps were heavy and definitely those of a man. In February of 1963 there was a late party in the building. After everybody had left, Clay went home secure in the knowledge that he alone possessed the key to the back door. The layout of the Octagon is such that nobody can hide from an inspection, so a guest playing a prank by staying on is out of the question.

At 3 A.M. the police called Clay to advise him that all lights at the Octagon were blazing and that the building was wide open. Mr. Woverton, the controller, checked and together with the police went through the building, turning off all lights once more. Everything was locked up again, in the presence of police officers.

At 7 A.M., however, they returned to the Octagon once more, only to find the door unlocked, the lights again burning. Yet, Clay was the only one with the key!

"Mr. Clay," I said, "after all these weird experiences, do you believe in ghosts?"

"No, I don't," Clay said, and laughed somewhat uneasily. He is a man of excellent educational background and the idea of accepting the uncanny was not at all welcome to him. But there it was. "Then how do you explain the events of the past couple of years?" "I don't," he said and shrugged. "I just don't have a rational explanation for them. But they certainly happened."

From the testimony heard, I am convinced that there are two ghosts in the Octagon, restlessly pacing the creaking old floors, vying with each other for the attention of the flesh-and-blood world outside.

There are the dainty footsteps of Colonel Tayloe's suicide daughter, retracing the walks she enjoyed but too briefly; and the heavy, guilt-laden steps of the father, who cannot cut himself loose from the ties that bind him to his house and the tragedy that darkened both the house and his life.

THE OCTAGON REVISITED

BACK IN 1965 I published a comprehensive account of the hauntings and strange goings-on at one of Washington's most famous houses. Frequently referred to as "the second White House" because it served in that capacity to President Madison during the War of 1812, the Octagon still stands as a superb monument to American architecture of the early nineteenth century. Most people hear more about the Pentagon than about the Octagon when referring to Washington these days, but the fact is that the Octagon is still a major tourist attraction, although not for the same reasons that brought me there originally. As a matter of fact, The American Institute of Architects, who own the building, were and are quite reluctant to discuss their unseen tenants. It took a great deal of persuasion and persistence to get various officials to admit that there was something amiss in the old building.

After my first account appeared in Ghosts I've Met, which Bobbs-Merrill published in 1965, I received a number of calls from people in Washington who had also been to the Octagon and experienced anything ranging from chills to uncanny feelings. I also found that the executives of The American Institute of Architects were no longer quite so unfriendly towards the idea of a parapsychologist investigating their famous old headquarters. They had read my account and found in it nothing but truthful statements relating to the history and psychic happenings in the house, and there really was nothing they could complain about. Thus, over the years I remained on good terms with the management of The American Institute of Architects. I had several occasions to test the relationship because once in a while there seemed to be a chance to make a documentary film in Washington, including, of course, the Octagon. It didn't come to pass because of the difficulties involved not with The American Institute of Architects but the more worldly difficulties of raising the needed capital for such a serious-minded film.

Originally I became aware of the potential hauntings at the Octagon because of a *Life* magazine article in 1962. In a survey of allegedly haunted houses, *Life* claimed that some visitors to the Octagon had seen a shadow on the spot where a daughter of Colonel Tayloe, who had built the house, had fallen to her death.

As far as I could ascertain at the time, there was a tradition in Washington that Colonel John Tayloe, who had been the original owner of the Octagon, had also been the grieving father of a daughter who had done the wrong thing marriage-wise. After she had run away from home, she had later returned with her new husband asking forgiveness from her stern father and getting short shrift. In desperation, so the tradition goes, she then flung herself from the third-floor landing of the winding staircase, landing on a spot near the base of the stairs. She died instantly. That spot, by the way, is one of those considered to be the most haunted parts of the Octagon.

A somewhat different version is given by Jacqueline Lawrence in a recent survey of Washington hauntings published by the Washington Post in October of 1969. According to Miss Lawrence, Colonel Tayloe had more than one daughter. Another daughter, the eldest one, had fallen in love with a certain Englishman. After a quarrel with her father, who did not like the suitor, the girl raced up the stairs and when she reached the second landing, went over the bannister and fell two flights to her death. This, then, would have been not a suicide but an accident. As for the other daughter, the one who had brought home the wrong suitor according to tradition, Miss Lawrence reports that she did not marry the man after all. Her father thought of this young Washington attorney as a man merely after his daughter's money and refused to accept him. This was especially necessary as he himself had already chosen a wealthy suitor for his younger daughter. Again an argument ensued, during which he pushed the girl away from him. She fell over that same ill-fated bannister, breaking her neck in the fall. This also according to Miss Lawrence was an accident and not suicide or murder. In addition to these two unfortunate girls, she also reports that a slave died on that same staircase. Pursued by a British naval officer, she threw herself off the landing rather than marry him. According to Miss Lawrence, the young man immediately leaped after her and joined her in death.

It is a moot question how easily anyone could fall over the bannister, and I doubt that anyone would like to try it as an experiment. But I wondered whether perhaps the story of the two girls had not in the course of time become confused into one tradition. All three deaths would have had to take place prior to 1814. In that year Washington was taken by the British, and after the burning of the White House, President Madison and his family moved temporarily into the Octagon. They stayed there for one full year, during which the Octagon was indeed the official White House.

Only after President Madison and his family had left the Octagon did accounts of strange happenings there become known. People in Washington started to whisper that the house was haunted. Allegedly, bells could be heard when there was no one there to ring them. The shade of a girl in white had been observed slipping up the stairway. The usual screams and groans associated with phantoms were also reported by those in the know. According to Miss Lawrence, seven years after the Civil War five men decided to stay in the house after dark to prove to themselves that there was nothing to the stories about the haunting. They too were disturbed by footsteps, the sound of a sword rattling, and finally, human shrieks. Their names, unfortunately, are not recorded, but they did not stay the night.

After some correspondence with J. W. Rankin, Director of the Institute, my wife, Catherine, and I finally started out for Washington on May 17, 1963. The beautiful Georgian mansion greeted us almost as if it had expected us. At the time we did not come with a medium. This was our first visit and I wanted to gain first impressions and interview those who actually had come in contact with the uncanny, be it visual or auditory. First I asked Mr. Rankin to supply me with a brief but concise rundown on the history of the house itself. It is perhaps best to quote here my 1965 report in "Ghosts I've Met."

Only one prior account of any unusual goings-on at the Octagon had come to my attention before my visit in 1963. The July 1959 issue of *The American Institute of Architects' Journal* contains a brief account of the long service record of a certain employee named James Cypress. Although Mr. Cypress himself had never seen any ghosts, he did report that there was an unusual occurrence at one time when his wife was ill and in need of a doctor. The doctor had reported that he had seen a man dressed in the clothes of about one hundred fifty years ago coming down the spiral staircase. The doctor looked at the stranger somewhat puzzled. At that instant the apparition dissolved into thin air, leaving the medical man even more bewildered. A short time before publication of "Ghosts I've Met". Joy Miller of the Associated Press wrote to me about the Octagon ghosts, adding a few more details to the story.

Legend has it that on certain days, particularly the anniversary of the tragic affair, no one may cross the hall at the foot of the stairway where the body landed without unconsciously going around an unseen object lying there.

The story of the bells that ring without due cause also is embroidered in this account.

Once, so a story goes, a skeptic leaped up and caught hold of the wires as they started to ring. He was lifted off the floor but the ringing kept on. To keep superstitious servants, the house was entirely rewired, and this apparently did the trick.

Of course, accounts of this kind are usually anonymous, but as a parapsychologist I do not accept reports no matter how sincere or authentic they sound unless I can speak personally to the one to whom the event has occurred.

When I started to assemble material for this book, I wondered what had happened at the Octagon since 1963. From time to time I keep reading accounts of the hauntings that used to be, but nothing startling or particularly new had been added. It became clear to me that most of these newspaper articles were in fact based on earlier pieces and that the writers spent their time in the research libraries rather than in the Octagon. In April of 1969 I contacted The American Institute of Architects again, requesting permission to revisit the Octagon, quietly and discreetly but with a medium. The new executive director, William H. Scheick, replied courteously in the negative: "The Octagon is now undergoing a complete renovation and will be closed to visitors until this work is completed. We hope the Octagon will be ready for visitors in early 1970. I am sorry that you and your guest will not be able to see the building when you are in Washington."

But Mr. Scheick had not reckoned with the persistence and flexibility of an erstwhile ghost hunter. I telephoned him and after we had become somewhat better acquainted, he turned me over to a research staff member who requested that I let him remain anonymous. For the purpose of this account, then, I will refer to him simply as a research assistant. He was kind enough to accompany us on a tour of the Octagon, when we managed to come to Washington, despite the fact that the house was in repair or, rather, disrepair.

The date was May 6, 1969; the day was hot and humid, as so many days in May are in Washington. With me was my good friend Ethel Johnson Meyers, whom I had brought to Washington for the purpose of investigating several houses, and Mrs. Nicole Jackson, a friend who had kindly offered to drive us around. I can't swear that Mrs. Meyers had not read the account of my earlier investigation of the Octagon. We never discussed it particularly, and I doubt very much that she had any great interest in matters of this kind, since she lives in New York City and rarely goes to Washington. But the possibility exists that she had read the chapter, brief as it is, in my earlier book. As we will see in the following pages, it really didn't matter whether she had or had not. To her, primary impressions were always the thing, and I know of no instance where she referred back to anything she had done before or read before.

When we arrived at the Octagon, we first met with the research assistant. He received us courteously and first showed us the museum he had installed in the library. We then proceeded through the garden to the Octagon building itself, which is connected with the library building by a short path. Entering the building from the rear rather than the imposing front entrance as I had in 1963, we became immediately aware of the extensive work that was going on inside the old building. Needless to say, I regretted it, but I also realized the necessity of safeguarding the old structure. Hammering of undetermined origin and workmen scurrying back and forth were not particularly conducive to any psychic work, but we had not choice. From noon to 1 o'clock was the agreed-upon time for us, and I hoped that we could at least learn something during this brief period. I urged Ethel to find her own bearings the way she always does, and the three of us followed her, hoping to catch what might come from her lips clairvoyantly or perhaps even in trance. Immediately inside the building, Ethel touched me, and I tried to edge closer to catch what came from her. She was quite herself and the impressions were nothing more than clairvoyant descriptions of what raced through her mind. We were standing in the room to the left of the staircase when I caught the name "Alice."

"What about Alice?" I asked. "Who is she?"

"I don't know. It just hit me."

"I won't tell you any more than that you should try to find your way around this general area we are in now, and upstairs as far as you feel like."

"Oh yes, my goodness, there's so many, they won't stay still long enough. There's one that has quite a jaw—I don't see the top of the face yet; just a long jaw."

"Man or woman?"

"Man."

"Is this an imprint from the past or is this a person?"

"From the past."

"Go over to this bannister here, and touch the bannister and see whether this helps you establish contact."

"I see a horse face."

"Is this part of his character or a physical impairment?"

"Physical impairment."

"What is his connection with this house?"

"I just see him here, as if he's going to walk out that door. Might have a high hat on, also. I keep hearing, 'Alice. Alice.' As if somebody's calling."

"Are there several layers in this house, then?"

"I would say there are several layers."

"Is there anything about this area we're standing in that is in any way interesting to you?" We were now in front of the fatal banister.

"Well, this is much more vivid. This is fear."

She seemed visibly agitated now, gripping the banister with both hands. Gently, I pried her loose and led her up a few steps, then down again, carefully watching her every move lest she join the hapless Tayloe girls. She stopped abruptly at the foot of the stairs and began to describe a man she sensed near the staircase— a phantom man, that is. Connected with this male ghost, however, was another person, Ethel indicated.

"Someone has been carried down these steps after an illness, and out of here. That's not the man, however. It seems to be a woman."

"What sort of illness?"

"I don't know. I just see the people carrying her down—like on a stretcher, a body, a sick person."

"Was this person alive at the time when she was carried down?"

"Alive, but very far gone."

"From where did she come?"

"I think from down here." Ethel pointed toward the spot beneath the bannister. "There is also a Will, but during this time I don't think Will is alive, when this happens. I also find the long-faced man walking around. I can see through him."

"Is he connected with the person on the stretcher?"

"I would say so, because he follows it." Then she added,

"Someone comes here who is still alive from that. Moved around."

"A presence, you mean?" She nodded. "This man with the horse face—what sort of clothes did he wear?"

"A formal suit with a long coat. Turn of the century or the twenties?"

"The nineteen-twenties?"

"Somewhere in here, yes."

"And the person on the stretcher—do you see her?"

"No, she's covered up. It is the woman I still see in here."

"Why don't you go up those stairs, to about the first landing."

"I am afraid of that, for some reason or other."

"Why do you suppose that is?"

"I don't like it."

"Did something happen in that area?"

"I don't know. I'm just getting a feeling as if I don't want to go. But I'll go anyway."

"See whether you get any more impressions in doing that!"

"I'm getting a cerebral heaviness, in the back of the head."

"Was somebody hurt there?"

"I would say. Or—stricken."

"What is the connection? Take one or two steps only, and see whether you feel anything further in doing this. You're now walking up the stairs to the first landing."

"Oh, my head. Whew!"

"You feel—?"

"Numb."

"We're not going further than the first landing. If it too difficult, don't do it."

"No. I'll take it for what it is." Suddenly, she turned. Don't push me!"

"Somebody's trying to push you?"

"Yes."

I didn't feel like testing the matter. "All right, come back here. Let us stand back of the first landing."

"I get a George, too. And Wood, and something else. I'm holding onto my head, that hurts, very badly."

"Do you know who is this connected with, the injury to the head?"

"It sounds like Jacques."

"Is he connected with this house in any official capacity?"

"Well, this is a definite ghost. He's laughing at me. I don't like it!"

"Can you get any name for this person?"

"Again I get Jacques."

"Did anything tragic ever happen here?"

"I would say so. I get two individuals here—the long-faced man, and a shorter-faced man who is much younger."

"Are they of the same period?"

"No."

"Where does the woman on the stretcher fit in?"

"In between, or earlier."

"What is this tragic event? What happened here?"

"I can hardly get anything. It feels like my brains are gone."

"Where do you think it happened? In what part of the building?"

"Here, of course, here."

"Did somebody die here? Did somebody get hurt?"

"According to my head, I don't know how anybody got through this. It is like blown off. I can't feel it at all. I have to put my hand up to find it."

"Are the presences still here?"

Instead of replying, Ethel put up her hands, as if warding off an unseen attack. "Oh, no!"

"Why did you just move like this? Did you feel anyone present?"

"Yes—as if somebody was trying to get hold of me, and I don't want that. I don't know how long I can take the head business, right here…"

"All right, we'll go down. Tell them, whoever might be present, that if they have to say something, they should say it. Whatever information they have to pass on, we are willing to listen. Whatever problem they might have."

Ethel seemed to struggle again, as if she were being possessed.

"There's something foreign here, and I can't make out what is being said."

"A foreign language?"

"Yes."

"What language is it?"

"I'm not sure; it's hard to hear. It sounds more Latin than anything else."

"A Latin language? Is there anything about this house that makes it different from any other house?"

"There's a lot of foreign influence around it."

"Was it used in any way other than as a dwelling?"

"There were séances in this place."

"Who do you think held them?"

"Mary."

"Who is this Mary?"

"She parted her hair in the middle. Heavy girl. I've got to put my hand up, always to my head, it hurts so."

"Do you get the names of the people involved in this horrible accident, or whatever it is that you describe, this painful thing?"

"That has to be Mary who's taken down the steps. I think it's this one."

"The tragedy you talk about, the pain…"

"It seems like it should be here, but it could have been somewhere else. I don't understand. There are two layers here."

"There may be many layers."

"There are so many people around here, it's so hard to keep them separate."

"Do you get the impression of people coming and going? Is there anything special about the house in any way?"

"I would say there is. The highest people in the land have lived here. I'm positively torn by the many things. Someone married here with the name of Alice. That has nothing to do with the head."

"Alice is another layer?"

"That's right."

"Mary has the injury to her head. Is the marriage of Alice later or earlier?"

"Much later." Then she added. "This house is terribly psychic, as it were—it is as if I have been able to find the easiest possible connections with a lot of people through what has been done here, psychically. There's a psychic circle around this place. From the past."

"Do you feel that these manifestations are still continuing?"

"I would say there are, yes. I don't know what all this rebuilding is doing to it, particularly when the painting starts. Has Lincoln had anything to do with this house? I feel that I see him here."

"What would be his connection with the house?"

"Nothing at all, but he's been her."

"Why would he be here?"

"I see an imprint of him."

"As a visitor?"

"I would say, yes. Some other high people have been here, too."

"As high as he?"

"That's right."

"Before him or after him?"

"After."

"What about before? Has anybody been as high as he here?"

"I would say so." Ethel, somewhat sheepishly, continued. "The man with the long face, he looks like Wilson!"

At that I raised my eyebrows. The mention of President Lincoln, and now Wilson, was perhaps a little too much name-dropping. On the other hand, it immediately occurred to me that both of these dignitaries must have been present at the Octagon at one time or other in their careers. Even though the Octagon was not used as a second White House after the disastrous War of 1812, it had frequently been used as a major reception hall for official or semiofficial functions. We do not have any record as to President Lincoln's presence or, for that matter, Wilson's but it is highly likely that both of these men visited and spent time at the Octagon. If these occasions included some festivities, an emotional imprint might very well have remained behind in the atmosphere and Ethel would, of course, pick that up. Thus her mention of Lincoln and Wilson wasn't quite as outlandish as I had at first thought.

For several minutes now I had noticed a somewhat disdainful smile on the research assistant's face. I decided to discontinue questioning Ethel, especially as it was close to 1 o'clock now and I knew that the assistant wanted to go to lunch.

I wondered whether any of the foregoing material made any sense to him. Frankly, I didn't have much hope that it did, since he had been honest enough to communicate his lack of faith in the kind of work I was doing. But he had been kind enough to come along, so the very least I could do was use his services such as they might turn out to be.

The name Alice meant nothing to him, but then he was tuned in on the history of the Octagon rather than Washington history in general. Later, at the Wilson House I realized that Ethel was in some peculiar way catapulting her psychic readings. It appeared that Alice meant a good deal in the history of President Wilson. What about Lincoln? The assistant shook his head.

"The family left the house about 1854, and I guess Lincoln was a Congressman then. He could have been here, but..."

"You're not sure?"

"I mean, he's not on the list that we have of people who have been here. I have no knowledge of it."

Colonel Tayloe died in 1854, and the house was owned by the family until after 1900 when the Institute bought it. But it was not occupied by the Tayloe family after the Colonel's death. I wondered why.

As to the names of the Tayloes' daughters, the research assistant wasn't very helpful either. He did have the names of some of the daughters, but he couldn't put his hands on them right now. He did not remember Mary. But, on reflection, there might have been.

I turned to Ethel. It was clear to me that the noise of the returning workmen, who had just finished their lunch hour, and the general tone of the conversation did not help to relax her. I thanked the assistant for his presence, and we left the building. But before we had walked more than a few steps, Ethel stopped suddenly and turned to me and said, "Somebody was murdered here, or badly wounded at least." She felt it was the woman on the stretcher. She was not completely sure that death had been due to murder, but it was certainly of a violent kind. I pointed at a portrait on the wall; the picture was that of Colonel Tayloe. Did Ethel recognize the man in the picture, I asked, without of course indicating who he was. Perhaps she knew anyway. She nodded immediately.

"That's the man. I saw him."

He was one of the men she had seen walking about with a peculiar tall hat. She was quite sure. The face somehow had stuck in her mind. Ethel then pointed at another portrait. It was a photograph of Mrs. Wilson. She too had been at the Octagon. Ethel felt the presence.

"Would this be 1958?" she asked somewhat unsure. The date seemed possible.

In evaluating Ethel's performance, I kept in mind that she had rarely if ever been wrong in pinpointing presences in haunted houses. Under the circumstances, of course, there was no possibility of Ethel going into full trance. Her contact with the entities was at the very best on the surface. Nevertheless, if three lady ghosts mentioned by Jacqueline Lawrence in her article had been present, then Ethel would surely have felt, seen, or otherwise indicated them. I am quite sure that Ethel never saw the article in the *Washington Post.* I am also equally sure that had she seen it, it would have made no difference to her, for she is a dedicated and honest medium. In the building itself she found her way to the psychic "hot spot" without my help, or in any way relying on my guidance. Had she been there before it would have made no difference, since the renovation had completely altered the impression and layout of the downstairs. I myself was hard put to find my way around, even though I had been to the Octagon on two previous occasions.

Thus, Ethel Johnson Meyers tended to confirm the original contention published by me in 1965. One girl ghost and one male ghost, daughter and father, would be the logical inhabitants of the Octagon at this time. Whether or not the entities themselves are aware of their plight is a moot question.

It appears to be equally difficult to ascertain the true nature of the girl's problem. Had she merely brought home a suitor whom her father did not like, or had she actually gotten married? Strange as it seems, the records are not clear in this case. What appears to be certain, at least to me, is her death by falling from the upper story. Ethel Johnson Meyers would not have picked up the "passing condition" had she not genuinely felt it. Furthermore, these impressions were felt by the medium on the very spot where traditionally the girl landed. Thus, Ethel was able to confirm the continuous presence of an unfortunate young woman in what used to be her father's house. Since the two Presidents whom the medium felt in some way attached to the house are hardly of the ghostly kind, it remains for Colonel Tayloe himself to be the man whose footsteps have been identified by a number of witnesses.

The American Institute of Architects no longer considers the Octagon the kind of museum it was before the renovation. It prefers that it be known primarily as their headquarters. Also, it is doubtful that the frequent parties and social functions that used to take place inside its walls will be as frequent as in the past, if indeed the Institute will permit them altogether.

If you are a visitor to the nation's capital and are bent on unusual sights, by all means include the Octagon in your itinerary. Surely once the renovation is completed there can be no reason—I almost said no earthly reason—for a visitor to be denied the privilege of visiting the American Institute of Architects. And as you walk about the Octagon itself and look up at the staircase perhaps wondering whether you will be as fortunate, or unfortunate as the case may be, as to see one of the two phantoms, remember that they are only dimly aware of you if at all. You can't command a ghost to appear. If you manage to wangle an invitation to spend the night, perhaps something uncanny might happen—but then again, it might not. What you can be sure of, however, is that I haven't "deghosted" the Octagon by any means even though a medium, Ethel Johnson Meyers, was briefly almost on speaking terms with its two prominent ghosts.

It remains to be seen, or heard, whether further psychic phenomena take place at the Octagon in the future.

8. THE HEADLESS GRANDFATHER

GROVER C. WAS ONE OF THOSE colorful old-timers you hardly see anymore these days, not even in the deep South. It wan't that Grover had any particular background in anything special, far from it; he was an untutored man who owed his success solely to his own willpower and an insatiable curiosity that led him places his education—or lack of it—would have prevented him from ever reaching.

He saw the light of day just before the turn of the century in rural North Carolina. At the age of nineteen he married for the first time, but his wife Fannie and the child she bore him both died from what was then called "childbed fever," or lack of proper medical treatment. He had not yet chosen any particular career for himself, but was just "looking around" and did odd jobs here and there. A year later he was married again, to a lady from Georgia who is still living. After their first girl was born, they moved to Columbus, Georgia, and Mr. C. worked in a local mill for a while. This didn't satisfy his drive, however, and shortly afterward he and his brother Robert opened a grocery store. The store did right well until "the Hoover panic," as they called it, and then they managed to sell out and buy a farm in Harris County.

Life was pretty placid, but after an accident in which he lost his daughter, Mr. C. moved back to Columbus and tried his hand at the grocery business once more. About this time, the restless gentleman met a lady from Alabama, as a result of which he became the father of an "extracurricular" little girl, in addition to his own family, which eventually consisted of a wife and nine children, two of whom are dead, the others still living.

When his second-born child died of an infectious disease, Mr. C. had his long-delayed breakdown, and for several years, he was unable to cope with his life. During those rough years of slow, gradual recuperation, his daughter Agnes ran the store for him and supported the family.

As his health improved and he began to return to a happier and more constructive outlook on life, he developed an interest in real estate. With what money he could spare, he bought and sold property, and before long, he did so well he could dispense with the grocery store.

Soon he added a construction business to his real estate dealings and was considered a fairly well-to-do citizen in his hometown. This status of course attracted a variety of unattached women and even some who were attached, or semi-detached, as the case may have been, and Mr. C. had himself a good time. Knowledge of his interest in other ladies could not fail to get to his wife and eventually he was given a choice by his wife: it was either her or them.

He picked them, or, more specifically, a lady next door, and for thirteen years he was reasonably faithful to her. Eventually she disliked living with a man she was no married to, especially when he happened to be married to someone else, even though he had bought her a cute little house of her own in Columbus. Mr. C. was not particularly happy about this state of affairs either, for he developed a penchant for drinking during those years. After they separated, the lady next door left town and got married.

Far from returning to the bosom of his family, now that the "other woman" had given him the gate, Grover looked elsewhere and what he found apparently pleased him. By now he was in his late sixties, but his vigorous personality wasn't about to be slowed down by so silly a reason as advancing age!

About 1962 he met a practical nurse by the name of Madeline, who turned out to be the opposite of what the doctor had ordered. After a particularly heavy argument, she kicked him in the nose. When it did not stop bleeding, she became alarmed and took him to the hospital. The family went to see him there even though his wife had not exactly forgiven him. But at this point it mattered little. Mr. C. also complained of pain in his side and the children firmly believed that the practical nurse had also kicked him in that area. Since he died shortly afterward, it was a moot question whether or not she had done so because Mrs. C's abilities no longer corresponded to her amorous expectations. The old gent certainly did not discuss it with his family. He was seventy when he died and Madeline was a mere sixty. Death was somewhat unexpected despite the fact Mr. C. had suffered from various ailments. During the days he had been alone in his room at the hospital. At first, he shared the room with another older man, but several days later a young man was sent in to be with him. The young man's complaint was that he had a lollipop stick stuck in his throat. There probably aren't too many young men with such a predicament in medical annals, and even fewer in Columbus, Georgia. The family found this mighty peculiar, even more so since the young man was a close relative of Madeline, the very practical nurse.

They complained to the hospital authorities and the young man was moved. It is not known whether the lollipop stick was ever removed from his throat, but chances are it was or we would have heard more of it. Young men with lollipop sticks in their throats either die from them or become sideshow attractions in the circus; the records show neither so it must be assumed that the lollipop stick got unstuck somehow somewhere along the line. At any rate, Mr. C. was now guarded by one of his children each night, the children taking turns.

They are firmly convinced that the practical nurse slipped her erstwhile benefactor some poison and that perhaps the boy with the lollipop stick stuck in his throat might have done her bidding and administered it to the old gent. This is a pretty sticky argument, of course, and hard to prove, especially as no autopsy was ever performed on Mr. C. But it is conceivable that Madeline made a discovery about her friend that could have induced her to speed his failure to recover and do so by any means at her command. She knew her way around the hospital and had ready access to his room. She also had equally ready access to his office and thereby hangs a strange tale.

On one of the infrequent occasions when Mr. C. slept at home, his estranged wife was making up the bed. This was five months before his demise. As she lifted the mattress, she discovered underneath it a heavy envelope, about six by ten inches in size, crammed full with papers. She looked at it and found written on it in Mr. C.'s large lettering, the words:

"This is not to be opened until I am dead. I mean good and dead, Daddy."

She showed the envelope to her daughter, Agnes, but put it

back since she did not wish to enter into any kind of controversy with her husband. Evidently the envelope must have been taken by him to his office sometime later, for when she again made his bed two weeks before his passing when he was still walking around, she found it gone. But there was a second, smaller envelope there, this one not particularly marked or inscribed. She left it there. A short time later Mr. C. was taken to the hospital. When Mrs. C. made the bed she found that the small envelope had also disappeared.

While the C.'s house in Columbus was not exactly a public place, neither was it an impregnable fortress, and anyone wishing to do so could have walked in at various times and quickly removed the envelope. As far as the office was concerned, that was even easier to enter and the family had no doubt whatever that Madeline took both envelopes for reasons best known to herself, although they could not actually prove any of it. At no time did the old gent say an unkind word about his Madeline, at least not to his children, preferring perhaps to take his troubles with him into the great beyond.

After his death, which came rather suddenly, the family found a proper will, but as Mr. C. had generously built homes for most of his children during his lifetime, in the 1950s, there was only a modest amount of cash in the bank accounts, and no great inheritance for anyone.

The will named Mrs. C. as executor, and as there was nothing to contest, it was duly probated. But the family did search the office and the late Mr. C.'s effects at the house for these two envelopes that were still missing. Only the wife and daughter Agnes knew of them, even though "nobody and everybody" had access to the house. The servants would not have taken them, and the safe was empty. As the old gent had occasionally slept in his office on a couch, the family looked high and low in his office but with negative results. The only thing that turned up in addition to the will itself was the neatly typed manuscript of a book of Biblical quotations. Mr. C. had been a serious Bible scholar, despite his uneducated status, and the quotes arranged by subject matter and source represented many thousands of hours of work. When his daughter Marie had seen him working on this project in 1962, she had suggested he have the scribbled notes typed up and she had prevailed upon her Aunt Catherine to undertake the job, which the latter did. Somewhat forlornly, Marie picked up the manuscript and wondered whether someone might not buy it and put a little cash into the estate that way.

The mystery of the disappearing envelopes was never solved. Even greater than the puzzle of their disappearance was the question about their content: what was in them that was so important that the old gent had to hide them under the mattress? So important that someone took them secretly and kept them from being turned over to the family, as they should have been?

Although there is no evidence whatever for this contention, Marie thinks there might have been some valuables left to Grover C.'s love child, the one he had with the lady from Alabama early in his romantic life.

At any rate, after several months of fruitless searches, the family let the matter rest and turned to other things. Grover C. would have gone on to his just reward, especially in the minds of his family, if it weren't for the matter of some peculiar, unfinished business. About a year after Grover's death, Lewis C., one of the sons of the deceased, as they say in the police records, was busy building a brick flower planter in his home in Columbus. This was one of the houses his father had erected for his children, and Mr. C., the son, had been living in it happily without the slightest disturbance. Lewis was thirty years old and the mystery of his father's disappearing envelopes did not concern him very much at this point. Here he was, at 4 o'clock in the afternoon, on a brisk March day in 1967, working on his planter. Giving him a hand with it, and handing him one brick after another, was a professional bricklayer by the name of Fred, with whom he had worked before. They were in the living room and Lewis was facing the back door, Fred the front door.

"A brick, please" said Lewis, without turning around.

No brick came. He asked again. Still no brick. He then looked up at his helper and saw him frozen to the spot, gazing at the front door.

"What's the matter, Fred?" he inquired. He had never seen Fred so frightened.

Finally, as if awakening from a bad dream, Fred spoke.

"I've just seen Mr. C.," he said, "big as life."

"But Mr. C. has been dead for a year," the son replied.

Fred had worked for Grover for many years and he knew him well.

"What did he look like?" the son inquired.

"White…light," Fred replied and then went on to describe the figure in white pants he had seen at the door. Although it was only the bottom half of a man, he had instantly recognized his late employer. Grover was bowlegged and the white pants facing him surely were as bowlegged as old Grover had been. There was no doubt about whose lower half it was that had appeared and then gone up in a puff again.

Lewis shook his head and went on with his work. But a short

time later he began to appreciate what Fred had experienced. In the middle of the night he found himself suddenly awake by reason of something in the atmosphere—undefinable, but still very real.

The lights in his bedroom were off, but he could see down the hallway. And what he saw was a man wearing a white shirt, dark pants…and…with no head. The headless gentleman was tiptoeing down the hallway toward him.

Lewis could only stare at the apparition which he instantly recognized as his late father, head or no head. When the ghost saw that Lewis recognized him, he took three leaps backward and disappeared into thin air.

Unfortunately, Catherine, Lewis' wife did not believe a word of it. For several months the subject of father's headless ghost could not be mentioned in conversation. Then in December 1968 Lewis and Catherine were asleep one night, when at about 2:30 A.M. they were both roused by the sound of heavy footsteps walking down the hall from the bedrooms toward the living room. As they sat up and listened with nary a heartbeat, they could clearly hear how the steps first hit the bare floor and then the carpet, sounding more muffled as they did. Finally, they resounded louder again as they reached the kitchen floor. Lewis jumped out of bed, ready to fight what he was sure must be an intruder. Although he looked the house over from top to bottom he found no trace of a burglar, and all the doors were locked.

In retrospect they decided it was probably Grover paying them a visit. But why? True, he had built them the house. True, they had some of his effects, especially his old pajamas. But what would he want with his old pajamas where he now was? Surely he could not be upset by the fact that his son was wearing them. They decided then that Grover was most likely trying to get their attention because of those envelopes that were still missing or some other unfinished business, but they didn't like it, for who would like one's headless father popping in the middle of the night?

But apparently Grover did not restrict his nocturnal visits to his son Lewis' place. His granddaughter Marie, who lives in Atlanta, had come to visit at her grandfather's house in the spring of 1968. The house had no city water but used water from its own well system. It was therefore necessary to carry water into the house from outside. On one such occasion, when she had just done this and was returning with an empty basin, Marie stepped into what looked like a puddle of water. She started to mop up the puddle only to find that the spot was actually totally dry. Moreover, the puddle was ice cold, while the water basin she had just carried was still hot. She found this most unusual but did not tell anyone about it. Within a matter of hours eight-year-old Randy reported seeing a man in a dark suit in the bathroom, when the bathroom was obviously empty.

Apparently the old gent liked children, for little Joel was playing the piano in his Atlanta home in February of 1969, when he heard the sound of shuffling feel approach. Then there was the tinkling of glasses and all this time no one was visible. Grover had always liked a shot and a little music.

Soon Marie began to smell carnations in her house when no one was wearing them or using any perfume. This lingered for a moment and then disappeared, as if someone wearing this scent was just passing through the house.

In 1967, her Aunt Mary came to visit her in Atlanta and the

conversation turned to the mysterious scent. "I'm glad you mentioned this," the aunt exclaimed, and reported a similar problem: both she and her husband would smell the same scent repeatedly in their own house, sometimes so strongly they had to leave the house and go out for some fresh air. But the scent followed them, and on one occasion "sat" with them in their car on the way to church on Sunday morning!

They weren't too sure whether it was more like carnations or just a funeral smell, but it surely was a smell that had no rational explanation. Then in 1968, Mary informed her niece that a new perfume had suddenly been added to their list of phenomena: this one was a spicy scent, like a man's after-shave lotion.

Not long after this report, Marie smelled the same sharp, men's perfume in her own house in Atlanta, in her den. This was particularly upsetting, because they had shut off that room for the winter and no perfume or anyone wearing it had been in it for months.

In 1969, she had occasion to visit her grandfather's house in Columbus once again. She found herself wandering into her late grandfather's old bedroom. She stopped at his dresser and opened the drawer. There she found her spicy scent: a bottle of Avon hair lotion he had used. None of her husband's eau de cologne bottles had a similar smell. This was it. But how had it traveled all the way to Atlanta? Unless, of course, Grover was wearing it.

Marie is a thirty-year-old housewife, has worked for years as a secretary to various business firms, and is married to a postal clerk. She was upset by her grandfather's insistence on continuing to visit his kinfolk and not staying in the cemetery as respectable folk are supposed to do, at least according to the traditional view of the dead.

Evidently Grover was far from finished with this life, and judging from the lively existence he had led prior to his unexpected departure from this vale of tears, he had a lot of energy left over. That, combined with a genuine grievance over unfinished business—especially the missing two envelopes—must have been the cause for his peripatetic visits. Marie decided not to wait for the next one, and went to see a card reader in Columbus. The card reader could tell her only that she had a restless grandfather who wished her well.

Unfortunately, even if the cause for Grover's continued presence could be ascertained, there was no way in which the missing envelopes could be legally recovered.

Marie tried, in vain, to get a local psychic to make contact with her grandfather. Finally, she turned her attention to the manuscript of Bible quotes. Perhaps it was the book he wanted to see published.

Whatever it was, she must have done the right thing, or perhaps all that talk about the headless grandfather had pleased the old gent's ego enough to pry him loose from the earth plane. At any rate, no further appearances have been reported and it may well be that he has forgotten about those envelopes by now, what with the attractions of his new world absorbing his interest.

Unless, of course, he is merely resting and gathering strength!

9. THE GHOSTLY ADVENTURES OF A NORTH CAROLINA FAMILY

TONI S. IS A YOUNG WOMAN of good educational background, a psychologist by profession, who works for a large business concern. She is not given to daydreaming or fantasizing. She is the daughter of Mrs. Elizabeth K., or rather the daughter of Mrs. K.'s second marriage. The thrice-married Mrs. K. is a North Carolina lady of upper middle-class background, a socially prominent woman who has traveled extensively.

Neither was the kind of person who pulls out a Ouija board to while away the time, or to imagine that every shadow cast upon the wall is necessarily a ghost. Far from it; but both ladies were taken aback by what transpired in their old house at the town of East La Porte, built on very old ground.

Originally built about fifty years ago, it was to be a home for Mrs. K.'s father who then owned a large lumber company, and the tract of timber surrounding the house extended all the way across the Blue Ridge Parkway. Undoubtedly an older dwelling had stood on the same spot, for Mrs. K. has unearthed what appears to be the remains of a much older structure. The house was renovated and a second story was built on about thirty-five years ago. At that time, her father had lost one leg as the result of an automobile accident, and retired from his lumber mill activities to East La Porte, where he intended to spend his remaining years in peace and quiet. He had liked the climate to begin with, and there was a sawmill nearby, which he could oversee. The house is a double-boxed frame house, perhaps fifty-by-fifty square, containing around fifteen rooms.

Mrs. K.'s family refer to it as the summer cottage, even though it was full-sized house; but they had other houses that they visited from time to time, and the house in East La Porte was merely one of their lesser properties. Downstairs there is a thirty-by-fifteen-foot reception room, richly carpeted with chestnut from Furnace Creek, one of the sawmills owned by the family. It was in this room that Mrs. K.'s father eventually passed on.

The house itself is built entirely from lumber originating in one of the family's sawmills. There was a center hall downstairs and two thirty-foot rooms, then there were three smaller rooms, a bath, a card room, and what the family referred to as a sleeping porch. On the other side of the center hall was a lounge, a kitchen, and a laundry porch. Running alongside the south and east walls of the house is a veranda. Upstairs is reached by a very gentle climb up the stairs in the middle of the floor, and as one climbs the steps, there is a bedroom at the head of the stairs. In back of the stairs, there are two more bedrooms, then a bathroom, and finally a storage room; to the left of the stairs are three bedrooms.

The attic is merely a structure to hold up the roof, and does not contain any rooms. There is a cellar, but it contains only a furnace. Although the acreage surrounding the house runs to about sixty acres, only three acres belong to the house proper. All around the house, even today, there is nothing but wilderness, and to get to the nearest town, East La Porte, one needs a car.

Mrs. K. enjoyed traveling, and didn't mind living in so many residences; in fact, she considered the house at East La Porte merely a way-station in her life. She was born in Alaska, where the family also had a sawmill. Her early years were spent traveling from one sawmill to another, accompanying her parents on business trips.

Under the circumstances, they were never very long in residence at the house in East La Porte. Any attempt to find out about the background of the land on which the house stood proved fruitless. This was Cherokee territory, but there is little written history concerning the time before the Cherokees. Anything remotely connected with physic phenomena was simply not discussed in the circles in which Mrs. K. grew up.

The first time Mrs. K. noticed anything peculiar about the house was after her father had passed away. She and her father had been particularly close, since her mother had died when she was still a small child. That particular day, she was sitting at her father's desk in the part of the house where her father had died. The furniture had been rearranged in the room, and the desk stood where her father's bed had previously been. Her father was on her mind, and so she thought it was all her imagination when she became aware of a distinctive sound like someone walking on crutches down the hall.

Since Mrs. K. knew for a fact that she was the only person in the house at the time, she realized that something out of the ordinary was happening. As the footsteps came closer, she recognized her father's tread. Then she heard her father's familiar voice say, "Baby." It came from the direction of the door. This gave her a feeling of great peace, for she had been troubled by emotional turmoil in her life. She felt that her late father was trying to console her, and give her spiritual strength.

Nothing happened until about a year later. It was August, and she had been in New York for awhile. As she was coming down the stairs of the house, she found herself completely enveloped with the fragrance of lilacs. She had not put any perfume on, and there were no lilacs blooming in August. No one was seen, and yet Mrs. K. felt a presence although she was sure it was benign and loving. A short time later, she was sitting at a desk in what used to be her father's study upstairs, thinking about nothing in particular. Again she was startled by the sound of footsteps, but this time they were light steps, and certainly not her father's. Without thinking, she called out to her daughter, "Oh, Toni, is that you?" telling her daughter that she was upstairs.

But then the steps stopped, and no one came. Puzzled, Mrs. K. went to the head of the stairs, called out again, but when she saw no one, she realized that it was not a person of flesh and blood who had walked upon the stairs.

During the same month, Mrs. K.'s daughter Toni was also at the house. Her first experience with the unseen happened that month, in an upstairs bedroom.

She was asleep one night when someone shook her hard and said, "Hey, you!" Frightened, she did not open her eyes, yet with her inner eyes, she "saw" a man of about fifty years of age. She was much too frightened to actually look, so instead she dove underneath the covers and lay here with her eyes shut. There was nothing further that night.

In the fall of the same year, Toni decided to have a pajama party and spent the night with a group of friends. Her mother had gone to bed because of a cold. Toni and her friends returned to the house from bowling at around 11:30. They were downstairs, talking about various things, when all of a sudden one of Toni's girlfriends said, "Your mother is calling you."

Toni went out into the hallway, turning on the lights as she approached the stairs. Footsteps were coming down the stairs, audible not only to her but to her two girlfriends who had followed her into the house. And then they heard a voice out of nowhere calling out, "Toni, it is time to go to bed." It was a voice Toni had never heard before.

She went up the stairs and into her mother's room, but her mother was fast asleep, and had not been out of bed. The voice had been a woman's, but it had sounded strangely empty, as if someone were speaking to her from far away.

The following years, Toni was married and left the house. Under the circumstances, Mrs. K. decided to sublease part of the house to a tenant. This turned out to be a pleasant woman by the name of Alice H. and her husband. The lady had been injured and was unable to go far up the mountain where she and her husband were building a summer home at the time. Although Mrs. K. and her new tenants were not associated in any way except that they were sharing the same house, she and Alice H. became friendly after a while. One afternoon, Alice H. came to Mrs. K.'s apartment in order to invite her to have supper with her and her husband that night. She knew that Mrs. K. was in her apartment at the time because she heard her light footsteps inside the apartment. When there was no reply from aside the apartment Alice was puzzled, so she descended to the ground floor, thinking that perhaps Mrs. K. was downstairs.

Sure enough, as she arrived downstairs, she saw a shadow of what she assumed to be Mrs. K.'s figure walking long the hallway. She followed this shadowy woman all he way from the ground floor guest room, through the bath into Mrs. K.'s bedroom, and then through another hallway and back to the bedroom. All the time she saw the shadowy figure, she also heard light footsteps. But when she came to the bedroom again, it suddenly got very cold and she felt all the blood rush to her head. She ran back to her husband in their own apartment, and informed him that there was a stranger in Mrs. K.'s rooms.

But there was no one in the house at the time except themselves, for Mrs. K. had gone off to Asheville for the day. The experience shook Alice H. to the point where she could no longer stand the house, and shortly afterward she and her husband left for another cottage.

In August of the same year, Toni S. returned to her mother's house. But now she was a married lady, and she was coming for a visit only. Her husband was a car dealer, in business with his father. At the time of the incident, he was not in the house. It was raining outside, and Toni was cleaning the woodwork in the house.

Suddenly her Pekinese dog came running down the stairs, nearly out of her mind with terror, and barking at the top of her lungs. Toni thought the dog had been frightened by a mouse, so she picked her up and proceeded up the stairs. But the dog broke away from her and ran behind the door. All of a sudden, Toni felt very cold. She kept walking down the hall and into the room, where there was a desk standing near the window. Someone was going through papers on her desk as if looking for a certain piece of paper, putting papers aside and continuing to move them! But there was no one there. No one, that is, who could be seen. Yet the papers were moving as if someone were actually shuffling them. It was 2 o'clock in the afternoon, and the light was fairly good.

Suddenly, one letter was pulled out of the piles of papers on the desk, as if to catch her attention. Toni picked it up and read it. It was a letter her father had sent her in February, at the time she got married, warning her that the marriage would not work out after all, and to make sure to call him if anything went wrong. Things had gone wrong since, and Toni understood the significance of what she had just witnessed.

At that very moment, the room got warm again, and everything returned to normal. But who was it standing at her desk, pulling out her father's letter? The one person who had been close to her while he was in the flesh was her grandfather.

During Toni's visit at the house, her husband, now her ex-husband, also had some uncanny experiences. Somebody would wake him in the middle of the night by calling out, "Wake up!" or "Hey you!" This went on night after night, until both Toni and her husband awoke around two in the morning because of the sound of loud laughing, as if a big party were going on downstairs.

Toni thought that the neighbors were having a party, and decided to go down and tell them to shut up. She looked out the window and realized that the neighbors were also fast asleep. So she picked up her dog and went downstairs, and as she arrived at the bottom of the stairs, she saw a strange light, and the laughing kept going on and on. There were voices, as if many people were talking all at once, having a social. In anger, Toni called out to them to shut up, she wanted to sleep, and all of a sudden the house was quiet, quiet as the grave. Evidently, Southern ghosts have good manners!

After her daughter left, Mrs. K. decided to sublease part of the house to a group of young men from a national fraternity who were students at a nearby university. One of the students, Mitchell, was sleeping in a double bed, and he was all alone in the house. Because the heat wasn't turned up, it being rather costly, he decided to sleep in a sleeping bag, keeping warm in this manner. He went to sleep with his pillow at the head of the bed, which meant due east, and his feet going due west. When he awoke, he found himself facing in the opposite direction, with his head where his feet should have been, and vice versa. It didn't surprise the young man though, because from the very first day his fraternity brothers had moved into the house, they had heard the sounds of an unseen person walking up and down the stairs.

One of their teachers, a pilot who had been a colonel in the Korean War, also had an experience at the house. One day while he was staying there, he was walking up the stairs, and when he reached about the halfway mark, someone picked him up by the scruff of his neck and pushed him up the rest of the way to the landing.

But the night to remember was Halloween Eve. Mrs. K. was in the house, and the night was living up to its reputation: it sounded as if someone wearing manacles were moving about. Mrs. K. was downstairs, sleeping in one of the bunk beds, and a noise came from an upstairs hall. This went on for about two hours straight. It sounded as if someone with a limp were pulling himself along, dragging a heavy chain. Mrs. K. was puzzled about this, since the noise did not sound anything like her father. She looked into the background of the area, and discovered that in the pre-colonial period, there had been some Spanish settlers in the area, most of whom kept slaves.

Toni S. takes her involvement with hauntings in stride. She has had psychic experiences ever since she can remember; nothing frightening, you understand, only such things as events before they actually happen—if someone is going to be sick in the family, for instance, or who might be calling. Entering old houses is always a risky business for her: she picks up vibrations from the past, and sometimes she simply can't stand what she feels and must leave at once.

But she thought she had left the more uncanny aspects of the hauntings behind when she came to New York to work. Somehow the wound up residing in a house that is one hundred ten years old.

After a while, she became aware of an old man who liked sitting down on her bed. She couldn't actually see him, but he appeared to her more like a shadow. So she asked some questions, but nobody ever died in the apartment and it was difficult for Toni to accept the reality of the phenomena under the circumstances. As a trained psychologist, she had to approach all this on a skeptical level, and yet there did not seem to be any logical answers.

Soon afterward, she became aware of footsteps where no one was walking, and of doors closing by by themselves, which were accompanied by the definite feeling of another personality present in the rooms.

On checking with former neighbors upstairs, who had lived in the house for seventeen years, Toni discovered that they too had heard the steps and doors closing by themselves. However, they had put no faith in ghosts, and dismissed the matter as simply an old structure settling. Toni tried her innate psychic powers, and hoped that the resident ghost would communicate with her. She began to sense that it was a woman with a very strong personality. By a process of elimination, Toni came to the conclusion that the last of the original owners of the house, a Mrs. A., who had been a student of the occult, was the only person who could be the presence she was feeling in the rooms.

Toni doesn't mind sharing her rooms with a ghost, except for the fact that appliances in the house have a way of breaking down without reason. Then, too, she has a problem with some of her friends; they complain of feelings extremely uncomfortable and cold, and of being watched by someone they cannot see. What was she to do? But then Toni recalled how she had lived through the frightening experiences at East La Porte, North Carolina, and somehow come to terms with the haunts there. No ordinary Long Island ghost was going to dispossess her!

With that resolve, Toni decided to ignore the presence as much as she could, and go about her business—the business of the living.

10. REBA'S GHOSTS

REBA B. IS A SENSITIVE, fragile-looking lady with two grown children. She was born in Kentucky, and hails from an old family in which the name Reba has occurred several times before. She works as a medical secretary and doctor's assistant, and nowadays shares her home with three cats, her children having moved away. Mrs. B., who is divorced, wondered whether perhaps she had a particular affinity for ghosts, seeing that she has encountered denizens of the other world so many times, in so many houses. It wasn't that it bothered her to any extent, but she had gotten used to living by herself except for her cats, and the idea of having to share her home with individuals who could pop in and out at will, and who might hang around her at times when she could not see them, did not contribute to her comfort.

Her psychic ability goes back to age three, when she was living with her grandparents in Kentucky. Even then she had a vivid feeling of presences all around her, not that she actually saw them with her eyes. It was more a sensitivity to unseen forces surrounding her—and awareness that as a child, she would see the figure of a man bending over her, a man she did not know. After a long period of this she wondered if she was dreaming, but in her heart she knew she was not. However, she was much too young to worry about such things, and as she grew up, her ability became part of her character, and she began to accept it as "normal."

This incident begins when she happened to be living in Cincinnati, already divorced. Her mother shared an old house with her, a house that was built around 1900; it had all the earmarks of the post-Victorian era: brass door knobs, little doorbells that were to be turned by hand, and the various trimmings of that age. The house consisted of three floors; the ground floor contained an apartment, and the two ladies took the second and third floor of the house. Reba had her bedroom on the third floor; it was the only bedroom up there situated in the middle of the floor.

One day she was coming up those stairs, and was approaching the window when she saw a man standing by it. He vanished as she came closer, and she gave this no more thought until a few days later. At that time she happened to be lying in bed, propped up and reading a book.

She happened to look up and saw a man who had apparently come up the stairs. She noticed his features fully: his eyes were brown, and he also had brown hair. Immediately she could sense that he was very unhappy, even angry. It wasn't that she heard his voice, but somehow his thoughts communicated themselves to her, mind to mind.

From her bed she could see him approach, walking out to a small landing and standing in front of her door. Next to her room was a storage room. He looked straight at Reba, and at that moment she received the impression that he was very angry because she and her mother were in that house, because they had moved into his house.

Although Reba B. was fully conscious and aware of what was

going on, she rejected the notion that she was hearing the thoughts of a ghost. But it did her no good; over and over she heard him say or think, "Out, out, I want you out, I don't want you here." At that moment he raised his arm and pointed outward, as if to emphasize his point. The next moment he was gone. Reba thought for a moment whether she should tell her mother whose bedroom was downstairs. She decided against it, since her mother had a heart condition and because she herself wasn't too sure the incident had been quite real. Also, she was a little frightened and did not want to recall the incident any more than she had to. After a while, she went off to sleep.

Not too long after that her daughter, who was then fourteen, and eleven-year-old son were home with her from school. It was a weekend, and she wanted the children to enjoy it. Consequently, she did not tell them anything about her ghostly experience. She had gone into the front storage room, when she thought she saw someone sitting on the boxes stacked in the storage area.

At first she refused to acknowledge it, and tried to look away, but when her gaze retured to the area, the man was still sitting there, quietly staring at her. Again she turned her head, and when she looked back, he was gone. The following weekend, her children were with her again. They had hardly arrived when her daughter returned from the same storage room asked, "Mother, is there someone sitting in there?" and all Reba could do was nod, and acknowledge that there was. Her daughter then described the stranger and the description matched what her mother had seen. Under the circumstances, Reba B. freely discussed the matter with her children. But nothing further was done concerning the matter, and no inquiries were made as to the background of the hourse. Summer came, and another spring and another summer, and they got into the habit of using the entrance at the side of the house. There were some shrubs in that area, and in order to enter the apartment in which they lived, they had to come up the stairs where they would have a choice of either walking into the living room on the second floor, or continuing on to the third floor where Reba's bedroom was. The tenant who had the ground floor apartment also had his own entrance.

One warm summer evening, she suddenly felt the stranger come into the downstairs door and walk up the stairs. When she went to check, she saw nothing. Still, she knew he was in the house. A few days passed, and again she sensed the ghost nearby. She looked, and as her eyes peered down into the hall, she saw him walking down the hall towards her. While she was thinking, "I am imagining this, there is no such thing as a ghost," she slowly walked toward him. As he kept approaching her, she walked right through him! It was an eerie sensation: for a moment she could not see, and then he was gone. The encounter did not help Reba to keep her composure, but there was little she could do about it.

Many times she sensed his presence in the house without seeing him, but early one evening, on a Sunday, just as it got dark, she found herself in the living room on the second floor of the house. She had turned on the television set, which was facing her, and she kept the volume down so as not to disturb her mother, whose room was on the same floor. She had altered the furniture in the room somewhat, in order to be closer to the television set, and there were two lounge chairs, one of which she used, and the other one close by, near the television set, so that another person could sit in it and also view the screen. She was just watching television, when she sensed the stranger come up the stairs again and walk into the living room. Next he sat down in the empty chair close to

Reba, but this time the atmosphere was different from that first encounter near the door of her room. He seemed more relaxed and comfortable, and Reba was almost glad that he was there keeping her company. Somehow she felt that he was glad to be in the room with her, and that he was less lonely because of her. He was no longer angry; he just wanted to visit.

Reba looked at the stranger's face and noticed his rather high-bridged nose. She also had a chance to study his clothes; he was wearing a brown suit, rather modern in style. Even though the house was quite old, this man was not from the early years, but his clothes seemed to indicate a comparatively recent period. As she sat there, quietly studying the ghost, she got the feeling that he had owned the house at one time, and that their living room had been the sitting room where the ghost and his wife had received people. Reba somehow knew that his wife had been very pretty—a fair-complexioned blonde, and she was shown a fireplace in the living room with a small love seat of the French Provincial type next to it, drawn up quite close to the fireplace. She saw this in her mind's eye, as if the man were showing her something from his past. At the same time, Reba knew that some tragedy had occurred between the ghost and his wife.

Suddenly, panic rose in Reba, as she realized she was sharing the evening with a ghost. Somehow her fears communicated themselves to her phantom visitor, for as she looked close, he had vanished.

As much as she had tried to keep these things from her mother, she could not. Her mother owned an antique covered casserole made of silver, which she kept at the head of her bed. The bed was a bookcase bed, and she used to lift the cover and put in receipts, tickets, and papers whenever she wanted.

One day, Reba and her mother found themselves at the far end of her bedroom on the second floor. Her bed was up against the wall, without any space between it and the wall. As the two ladies were looking in the direction of the bed, they suddenly saw the silver casserole being picked up, put down on the bed, turned upside down and everything spilled out of it. It didn't fly through the air, but moved rather slowly, as if some unseen force were holding it. Although her mother had seen it, she did not say anything because she felt it would be unwise to alarm her daughter; but later on she admitted having seen the whole thing. It was ironic how the two women were trying to spare each other's feelings—yet both knew that what they had witnessed was real.

The ghost did not put in any further appearances after the dramatic encounter in the living room. About a year later, the two ladies moved away into another old house far from this one. But shortly before they did, Reba's mother was accosted on the street by a strange middle-aged lady, who asked her whether she was living in the house just up the street. When Reba's mother acknowledged it, the lady informed her the house had once belonged to her parents. Were they happy in it, Reba's mother wanted to know. "Very happy," the stranger assured her, "Especially my father." It occurred to Reba that it might have been he who she had encountered in the house; someone so attached to his home that he did not want to share it with anyone else, especially flesh-and-blood people like her mother and herself.

The new home the ladies moved into proved "alive" with unseen vibrations also, but by now they didn't care. Reba realized that she had a special gift. If ghosts wanted her company, there was little she could do about it.

She had a friend who worked as a motorcycle patrolman, by the name of John H. He was a young man and well-liked on the force. One day he chased a speeder—and was killed in the process. At the time, Reba was still married, but she had known John for quite a few years before. They were friends, although not really close ones, and she had been out of touch with him for some time. One morning, she suddenly sensed his presence in the room with her; it made no sense, yet she was positive it was John H. After a while, the presence left her. She remarked on this to her mother and got a blank stare in return. The young man had been killed on the previous night, but Reba could not have known this. The news had come on the radio just that morning, but apparently Reba had had advance news of a more direct kind.

Reba B. shared her interest in the occult with an acquaintance, newscaster Bill G. In his position as a journalist, he had to be particularly careful in expressing an opinion on so touchy a subject as ESP. They had met a local restaurant one evening, and somehow the conversation had gotten around to ghosts.

When Mr. G. noticed her apprehension at being one of the "selected" ones who could see ghosts, he told her about another friend, a young medium who had an apartment not far away. One evening she walked out onto her patio, and saw a man in old-fashioned clothes approach her. The man tried to talk to her, but she could not hear anything. Suddenly he disappeared before her eyes. The young lady thought she was having a nervous breakdown, and consulted a psychiatrist; she even went into a hospital to have herself examined, but there was nothing wrong with her. When she returned to her home and went out onto the patio again, she saw the same ghostly apparition once more. This time she did not panic, but instead studied him closely. When he disappeared she went back into her apartment, and decided to make some inquiries about the place. It was then that she discovered that a long time ago, a man of that description had been hanged from a tree in her garden.

"These things do happen," Bill G. assured Reba, and asked her not to be ashamed or afraid of them. After all, ghosts are people too. Since then, Reba had come to terms with her ghostly encounters. She has even had an experience with a ghost cat—but that is another story.

11. THE GHOSTS
IN THE BASEMENT

MARY LIVES IN ATLANTA, GEORGIA, a quiet woman who speaks with a charming southern accent and is rather conservative in her way of life. Even her special talent of being able to read the tarot cards for her friends used to be an embarrassment to her because of her religion and because of what the neighbors might say if they found out, not to mention the fact that everyone would want a reading from her.

At the time I met her she had two lovely daughters, Katie, a 15-year-old, and Boots, who went to college. On the day of Halloween, 1962, she and her girls had moved into an attractive 18-year-old house in Atlanta. It stood in a quiet suburban neighborhood amid other small homes of no particular distinction. Not far from the house are the tracks of a railroad which is nowadays used only for freight. Famous old Fort McPherson is not far away; during the Civil War one of the bloodiest engagements was fought on this spot.

The house has two levels; at street level, there is a large living room which one enters from the front side of the house, then there are three bedrooms, and on the right side of the house, a den leading into a kitchen. From one of the bedrooms a stair secured by an iron railing leads into the basement. There is a closet underneath the stairs. In back of the house there is a large patio and there are also outside stairs leading again into the basement. Only the right-hand third of the basement area is actually used by the family, a laundry room occupies most of the space and a wall seals it off from the undeveloped "dirt" area of the basement.

The house itself feels cozy and warm, the furniture is pleasant and functional, and if it weren't for some unusual events that had occurred in the house, one might never suspect it of being anything but just another ordinary suburban home.

Soon after they had moved in, Mary and her daughters knew there was something very odd about the house. She would wake up in the middle of the night because she heard someone digging down in the basement. She thought this entirely out of the question, but when the noise persisted night after night, she was wondering whether the neighbors might be putting in a water pipe. After a while, she decided to find out who was doing the digging. She left her bed and went downstairs, but there was nothing to be seen. There were no rats or mice which could have caused the strange noise. There was no freshly turned up dirt either. Their neighbors weren't doing any digging. Even more mysterious, Mary and her two daughters kept hearing the noise of someone trying to break into the house, always at two in the morning. And when they checked there was never anyone there. They called the police but the police failed to turn up any clues. Mary installed heavy bolts inside the front and rear doors, but the day she returned from an errand to an empty house she found the heavy bolts ripped away by unseen hands.

At the time Mary was estranged from her doctor husband, and she was afraid to discuss the strange phenomena with him, since he put no stock into psychic phenomena and might have taken advantage of the information to have Mary declared in need of psychiatric treatment. Mary was in the habit of taking afternoon naps but now her naps kept being disturbed by an unseen person entering the house, walking through it as if he or she knew it well, and sometimes even running the water or flushing the toilet! Often, when she was doing her laundry in the basement she would clearly hear footsteps overhead, then the sound of drawers being opened and shut and water being run. But when she checked, there was no one about and nothing had changed.

At first she kept the disturbing news from her daughters but soon discovered that the children had also heard the strange noises. In addition, Katie had felt a pair of hands on her during the night when she knew she was alone in her room. Even in plain daylight such heavy objects as books began to disappear and reappear in other places as if someone were trying to play a game with them. At that time Boots, the older girl, was at college and when she came back from school she had no idea what her sister and mother had been through recently in the house. So it was a shock for her to hear someone using a typewriter in the basement when they all knew that there was no one there and no typewriter in the house. The family held a conference and it was decided that what they had in the house was a ghost, or perhaps several. By now they had gotten used to the idea, however, and it did not frighten them as much as before.

One night Katie was asleep when she awoke with the feeling she was not alone. As she opened her eyes she saw standing by her bedside a shadowy figure. Since her mother was in the other bedroom, she knew that it could not have been her.

Soon, Mary and her girl realized that they weren't dealing with just one ghost. On several occasions the quick footsteps of a child were also heard along with the heavier footsteps of an adult. Then someone seemed to be calling out to them by name. One day in January 1968 when they had gotten accustomed to their unseen visitors Mary awoke to the sound of music coming from the kitchen area. She investigated this at once but found neither a radio nor any other reason for the music that could be accepted on a rational basis. She returned to bed and tried to ignore it. Just then two sets of footfalls reached her ears right through the covers. One set of feet seemed to turn to toward her daughter Katie's room, while the other pair of feet came right toward her bed, where they stopped. Something ice cold then seemed to touch her. She screamed in fear and jumped from her bed and this apparently broke the phenomenon and again there was no one about.

Mary began to wonder who was the person in the household who made the phenomenon possible, because she knew enough about psychic phenomena to realize that someone had to be the medium. One night she received the answer. She awakened to the sound of a voice coming from her daughter Katie's room. A female voice was saying a phrase over and over and Katie was answering by repeating it. She could clearly hear "golden sand," spoken in a sweet, kindly voice and her daughter Katie repeating it in a childish voice totally different from her normal adult tone. Then she heard Katie clap her hands and say, "Now what can I do?" When Mary entered Katie's room she saw her daughter fast asleep. When questioned the next day about the incident, Katie remembered absolutely nothing. But the incidents continued.

One day Katie saw a woman in her forties, and felt someone fondling her hair. It seemed a kind gesture and Katie was not afraid. By now Mary wondered whether she herself might not be the person to whom the phenomena occurred rather than just her daughter. She had always had psychic ability so she decided to test this potential mediumship within her. Relaxing deeply in an effort to find out who the ghost was and what the ghost wanted in the house, Mary was able to hear with her inner voice the psychic message sent out from the woman. Over and over again she heard the phrase spoken within her—"I need your help to cross the stream!" Several days later she heard the same female voice whisper in her ear, "I need your help!" "Where are you?" Mary said aloud. "In the basement, in the dirt," the voice answered. Soon Mary realized there was another ghost in the house, this one male. Mary woke from an afternoon nap because she heard someone come through the front door. She sat up and yelled at the unseen presence to go away and leave her alone. But a man's gruff voice answered her. "She can see me!" But Mary did not see anyone. Still, she become more and more convinced that the man was angry at her for having paid attention to the female ghost and Mary wondered whether the two of them had a connection. Mary called on sincere friends to form a "psychic rescue circle," that is to try to make contact with the restless ghosts and, if possible, send them away. It didn't help. Soon after, Mary heard the pleading voice again, "I need you. Come to the basement." Mary then went to the basement where she said a prayer for the departed. Whether the prayer did it, or whether the ghosts had finally realized that they were staying on in a house that belonged to another time, there were no further disturbances after that.

12. THE GHOST IN THE PINK BEDROOM

THE AREA AROUND CHARLOTTESVILLE, Virginia, abounds with haunted houses, which is not surprising since this was at one time the hub of the emerging young American republic. There was a time when the American government had its capital, if only briefly, in Charlottesville and prior to the Revolution, the large landowners had built many magnificent manor houses which still dot the area. Much history and much tragedy has occurred in some of them, so it is not surprising to find that the reports of strange goings-on in the area are comparatively plentiful. One such house is the property of Colonel Clark Lawrence and his family, known as Castle Hill. It is considered one of the historical landmarks of the area and while it is not open to visitors, especially those looking for the ghost, it is conceivable that prior arrangements with the owners could be made for a student of history to have a brief visit. If this is diplomatically handled, the chances of being allowed to visit are good.

The main portion of the house was built by Dr. Thomas Walker in 1765, but additions were made in 1820. The original portion was made of wood, while the additions were of brick. These later changes executed under the direction of the new owner, Senator

William Cabell Rives, gave Castle Hill its majestic appearance. Senator Rives had been American ambassador to France and was much influenced in his tastes by French architecture. This is clear when one sees the entrance hall with its twelve-foot ceilings and the large garden laid out in the traditional French manner.

On the ground floor, to the rear, there is a suite of rooms which has a decidedly feminine flavor. This is not surprising since they were the private quarters of a later owner, Amelie Rives, an author and poet whose body lies buried in the family plot on the grounds. In this suite there is a bedroom called the pink bedroom, which is the center of ghostly activities. Whenever guests have been assigned to sleep in this room, they invariably complain of disturbances during the night. Writer Julian Green, a firm skeptic, left the next morning in great hurry. Amelie Rives herself spoke of a strange perfume in the room, which did not match any of her own scents. The ghostly manifestations go back a long time, but no one knows exactly who is attached to the room.

From the testimony of various guests, however, it appears that the ghost is a woman, not very old, rather pretty, and at times playful. Her intentions seem to be to frighten people using the room. Curiously, however, a few guests have slept in it without being aroused by uncanny noises or footsteps. Legend has it that those the lady ghost likes may sleep peacefully in "her" bedroom, while those she does not like must be frightened out of their wits.

I visited the bedroom in the company of sensitive Virginia Cloud, who had been there many times before. Curiously, I felt the vibrations of another presence, a fine, almost gentle person, but I could not see anyone. Nevertheless, I realized that I was not alone in the room, and Miss Cloud also felt that we were being observed by the unseen former owner of the place.

During the Revolutionary War, British General Banastre Tarleton and his troops occupied Castle Hill. The then owner, Dr. Walker, served them breakfast on June 4, 1781, and in the course of his hospitality delayed them as long as he could so that Jefferson, then in nearby Charlottesville, could make good his escape from the British. Whether or not one of the ladies played any significant part in this delaying action is not known, but I suspect that there is involvement of this kind connected with the appearance of the ghostly lady at Castle Hill. It was not uncommon for the women of the Revolutionary period to use their charms on the British, in order to further the cause of the revolution. Several such instances are known, and it must be said for the gallantry of the British officers, that they did not mind the intrigues of the American Colonial ladies at all.

13. THE "PRESENCE" ON THE SECOND-FLOOR LANDING

SOMEWHERE BETWEEN WASHINGTON and Baltimore is a small community called Sykesville. It is a little bit closer to Baltimore than in it is to Washington, and most of the people who live there work in Baltimore. Some don't work at all. It is not what you might call a poor community but, to the contrary, is one of the last remaining strongholds of the rural hunting set whose main occupation and pride were their farms and minor houses.

Howard Lodge was built there in 1774 by Edward Dorsey. Tradition has it that it was named Howard Lodge when Governor Howard of Maryland stayed in it during the period in which the United States became independent. Tax records seem to indicate that it was owned at one time by relatives of Francis Scott Key, the author of our national anthem. Key himself visited Howard Lodge and carved his name in one of the upstairs window sills, but unfortunately, the windows were later destroyed by storms.

The house consists of two stories and is made of brick imported from England. The attic and roof beams were made by hand from chestnut wood and are held fast by pegs driven their full length. Today's owners, Mr. and Mrs. Roy Emery, have made some changes, especially in the attic. At one time the attic was two stories high, but it has been divided into storage rooms above the beams and finished rooms below. At the turn of this century dormer windows were installed by a previous owner, a Mrs. Mottu of Baltimore. The oldest part of the house is the thick-walled stone kitchen downstairs. On the ample grounds there is an old smoke-house and a spring house, both dating from the original period when the house was built. Surrounded by tall trees, the estate is truly European in flavor, and one can very well imagine how previous owners must have felt sitting on their lawn looking out into the rolling hills of Maryland and dreaming of past glory.

The house has been furnished in exquisite taste by its present owners, the Emerys. Mr. Emery is an attorney in Baltimore, and his wife, a descendant of very old French nobility, saw service as a nurse in the late unlamented French-Indochina campaign. The furnishings include period pieces assembled with an eye towards fitting them into the general tone of the house, and French heirlooms brought into the house by Mrs. Emery. There isn't a piece out of key at Howard Lodge, and the house may well serve as an example to others who would live in eighteenth-century manor houses.

In 1967 I appeared on Baltimore television. Shortly after my appearance I received a letter from Mrs. Emery, in which she asked me to have a look at Howard Lodge and its resident ghosts. It would appear that she had several, and that while they were not malicious or mischievous, they nevertheless bore investigation if only to find out who they were and what they wanted.

Long before Mrs. Emery had heard of me, she had invited two men, who were aware of the existence of ghosts, to come to the house. They were not private investigators or apprentice ghost-

hunters, to be sure—simply two gentlemen interested in the supernatural. Barry and Glenn Hammond of Washington, D.C., coming
to the house as friends, reported seeing a gentleman outside looking toward the house. The gentleman in question was not of this
world, they hastily explained. They knew all about such personalities since they were accustomed to distinguishing between the
flesh-and-blood and the ethereal kind. The Emerys had other
guests at the time, so the two gentlemen from Washington were not
as much at liberty to speak of the resident ghosts as if they had
come alone. While they were wandering about the house in search
of other phantoms, Mrs. Emery busied herself with her guests. On
leaving, however, the Hammonds happily informed Mrs. Emery
that Howard Lodge had not just two ghosts—as the Emerys had
surmised—but a total of five. They left it at that and went back to
Connecticut Avenue.

Jacqueline Emery was not particularly overtaken with worry.
She was born Countess de Beauregard, and as with many old aris-
tocratic families, there had been a family specter and she was quite
familiar with it while growing up. The specter, known as the White
Lady, apparently can be seen only by members of the de
Montrichard family, who happened to be related to Mrs. Emery.
No one knows who the White Lady is, but she appears regularly
when a member of the family is about to die, very much as an
Irish banshee announces the coming of death. There may be a relationship there since so many old French families are also of Celtic
origin.

In 1969 my wife and I met Mrs. Emery's uncle, the Baron Jean
Bergier de Beauregard, who lives with his family it Chateau de
Villelouet in the heartland of France. The Baron readily confirmed

that many members of the Beauregard family have indeed shown the ability of second sight, and that psychic occurrences were not particularly upsetting to any of them. They took it in their stride. Jacqueline Emery has inherited this particular talent also. She frequently knows what is in the mail or what phone calls are about to be made to her, and she is aware of the future in many small ways, but she takes it as part of her character. Nevertheless, it indicates in all the Beauregards a natural vein of psychic ability, and it is that psychic ability that made the appearances at Howard Lodge possible, in my view.

Jacqueline Emery herself has more than a casual acquaintance with ESP. When I asked her to recall any incidents of a psychic nature prior to coming to Howard Lodge, she thought for a while and then reported a startling incident that occurred to her in December of 1944, when she was living in Germany.

For some reason I had gone to a village near Munich with a woman who wanted to buy eggs and chicken and also pick up some apples in the basement of a home she owned and had rented to a family from either Düsseldorf or Köln. I believe its name was Kaiserbrunn. A Mrs. Schwarz was renting.

Mrs. Kolb, with whom I had come, wanted me to go to the village with her, but for some reason I excused myself and went in quest of Mrs. Schwarz. She was in the dining room, busily writing letters. For some unknown reason I asked her what she was writing. It was odd because, at twenty, I was very shy. She then told me that she was sending farewell letters to her husband and children. She had, I noticed then, in front of her, some pills, which she said were poison. Upon my asking her she unfolded the following story:

She feared that her husband, a university professor, had been killed and their home demolished in a recent bombing of either of the cities I mentioned above. One of her sons was on the French front and hadn't been heard of for quite a period of time. Two other sons were on the Russian front, and she had no news from them either.

Perhaps worst of all, her daughter Lütte Paschedag, her two small children and their nurse, Schwester Margarethe, had supposedly left Potsdam several days before to come and stay with her and had not been heard from. News had been on the radio of several trains from the direction of Berlin being attacked and many deaths having ensued.

For some unexplained reason, I took her in my arms (I'd never seen her before) and promised her that her daughter, the nurse and the children were very close to Kaiserbrunn, that Hänsel, the one on the French front would be home within a week and stay for Christmas, that Professor Schwarz would call her up during the week, that their home had only been partly damaged, and that the two other sons and the son-in-law would write. One, Wolfgang, would be home for Christmas; the other was a doctor and I didn't think he could be spared for the holiday. Upon hearing me out, she fainted. She came to and together we burned the pills and letters. There was a knock at the door, it was Lütte, the two children and the nurse. Hänsel came the following week, Wolfgang was home for Christmas. Professor Schwarz called up two days after my visit, and the doctor wrote before Christmas. She was kind enough to send Hänsel to Munich to tell me and invite me to be with them for Christmas, which I did.

On June 11, 1969, I finally managed to come out to Howard

Lodge. Roy Emery picked me up in Baltimore and drove me to his house. Present were not only his wife but their two daughters, both college students. Ariane the elder, is an avid reader of mine and wants to devote herself to psychic studies if all goes well. Proudly, Jacqueline Emery showed me about the house and around the grounds while there was still enough light to see everything. While we were walking I learned further details about Howard Lodge. For one thing, it appeared that Jerome Bonaparte had actually been to the house while he was courting Mrs. Patterson, whom he later married. Not three miles away from Howard Lodge was the estate of the Pattersons, where Napoleon's brother lived out his life in peace and harmony. All around us was plantation country, and what little was left of the old plantations could still be seen in the area. "We now have only two hundred acres," Mrs. Emery explained, "but when we bought the property it was part of five hundred acres, and a hundred years ago it was about seven or eight hundred acres. I imagine that in the beginning it must have been about two thousand acres. That's what the plantations around here were like." Before I went into the matter of the hauntings properly, I wanted to learn as much as possible about the house itself, its background, its structure, and since Mrs. Emery already knew these facts I saw no reason not to discuss them.

"Was this the plantation house, actually?" I asked.

"It must have been, yes. And it is a rather formal house, which is typical of the English houses, with the hall going all the way through the house, and two rooms deep on either side. The kitchen must have been an addition later, even though it is old."

"There are four rooms downstairs?"

"There are more than that, but it is two rooms deep on either side of the hall. You see, here you have the living room and the music room, my husband's library, and the dining room. The dining room has been extended going east-west because the hall doesn't go all the way through to the door; the partition has been removed."

"And upstairs?"

"Upstairs, there are six bedrooms, and then the attic, which I will show you, was a two-story one. Now we've made it a third floor, with still a large attic on top."

"So it's actually a three-level house?"

"Well, we have the basement, we have this floor, the second floor, the third floor, and the attic; that's five stories."

"How long ago did you come here?"

"It will be ten years in December. We moved in here in 1959. The house had been lived in by hillbillies, and horribly mistreated. The kitchen, through which you came in, had pigs, with litters. This room was used—the various corners were used instead of bathrooms. It had a couch that was full of rats. The rats were so used to people that they didn't move when you came in. It was full of flies and fleas and rats and mice and smells, and chewing gum on the floors. And Roy and I spent about a month, on our knees, on this very floor, trying to remove all of this. All the walls were covered with six to seven layers of wallpaper, which were removed, and then I painted. Of course the hard part was removing the paper. Each time there had been a draft in the room, due to some hole in the masonry or something, they had put on another layer of wallpaper, thus cutting off, or hiding, the problem, rather than doing anything about it. And so forth!"

"Were they squatters or had they bought it?"

"They had bought it because they had had a farm on what is

now Friendship Airport. Needless to tell you, it was a very nice thing to have. They bought this house from a man who worked in a bank in Washington. They bought it cash."

"But they didn't know how to live."

"Oh, no! See, they used a house as you would squeeze a lemon; after there was nothing left, they left and abandoned the house— went to another one. The time had come for them to leave; they had been here seven years, and it was going to pot. The plumbing was completely shot. The heating system was so dangerous that the electrician said, 'You really must believe in God'; and everything about like that."

"And you took it over then and restored it?"

"Yes, and everybody told us we were absolutely crazy. We spent the first month, five of us, in one room. I had disinfected that room, working in it for a month."

"You have three children?"

"Yes. And Chris was only two. And—well, we are still working on it."

I decided to come to the point.

"When was the first time you noticed anything unusual anywhere?"

"It was when I became less busy with doing things in the house. You know, when you are terribly busy you don't have time to realize what's going on. Three years ago I became aware of a man on the landing. I know it is a man, though I have never seen him. I'm absolutely convinced that he's a man in either his late forties or early fifties, and in addition, he's from the eighteenth century because in my mind's eye I can see him."

"Was there anything for the first seven years of your occupancy here?"

"I cannot recall. Except possibly some vague sensation about steps going from the second to the third floor."

"Noises?"

"Oh yes, you always have the feeling somebody's going up the steps. Always. We've always taken it for granted it was because it was an old house, but since we have rugs I still hear steps."

"Now, what were the circumstances when you felt the man on the stairs? On the landing, I mean."

"Well, I was going to my room, on the second floor, and you have to go through the landing. This is the only way to go to that room. And then suddenly I had to stop, because he was there."

"Did you feel cold?"

"No, I just felt he had to move and he wasn't going to move, and eventually he did, but he wasn't aware of me as fast as I was of him."

"What time of day was that?"

"Evening. It's always dusk, for some reason. You see, the landing has a southern exposure, which may have something to do with it, and it's always very sunny during the day."

"After this first experience, did you have more?"

"Oh yes, often. For quite a while he was constantly there."

"Always on that spot?"

"Always on the landing. You see, the landing has a very good vantage point, because nobody can go upstairs or downstairs without going through it."

"Then would you say somebody might watch from that spot?"

"You can see everything—originally the lane was not what you came through, but at the front of the house. From the landing you have a perfect command of the entire lane."

After this first experience three years ago did you ever see him, other than the way you describe?"

"No. Although I have to be very careful when I say that because after a while, as you well know, it is difficult to separate something you see in your mind from something you see physically. Because I feel that I could touch him if I tried, but I never have. Even though I'm not afraid of him, I still don't feel like it."

"Did you ever walk up the stairs and run into something?"

"A wall. Sometimes I feel that there is a partition or something there."

"Something that you have to displace?"

"Yes. But then I wait until it displaces itself, or I move around it. But somehow I know where it is because I can move around it."

"Have you ever seen anything?"

"Often. On the landing."

"What does it look like?"

"Fog. And I always think it's my eyes."

"How tall is it?"

"Frankly I have never thought about it, because I will blink a few times. I've always thought it was me. You see, it's very foggy here, outside. But then I saw it in several rooms."

"Did you ever smell anything peculiar…."

"Yes, I often do. There are some smells in this house and they often take me back to something, but don't know what."

"Do you ever hear sounds that sound like a high-pitched voice, or a bird?"

"Bird, yes. Very often."

"Where do you hear that? What part of the house?"

"Never on this floor. Upstairs."

"Have there been any structural changes in the house?"

"I think the landing."

"Only the landing? How was it affected?"

"We changed one partition, for it was much too illogically altered to have been something that existed when the house was built. The way we found it, it couldn't have been that way because it was ridiculous. Anybody with a hoop skirt, for instance, or a wide dress, could never have managed the top of the steps onto the landing with the partition the way it was there. We changed it, and I will show you because the seam is in the floor. We were told that the landing had been changed, and for some reason everything is around that landing."

"You mean changed back to what it was originally, or changed?"

"We don't know, because we don't know how it was."

"Did you widen it or narrow it?"

"We widened it."

"Now, since living in this house have you ever had odd dreams? Have you felt as if a person were trying to communicate with you?"

"Yes. Often."

"Will you talk about that?"

"Only that I'm rather ashamed, that I usually try to block it out."

"Well, do you ever get any feeling of the communicators?"

"Because I'm negative I don't think there is any actual communication, but I've often been aware of someone even coming in the room where I am."

"How does this manifest itself?"

"I'm aware of a shadow. With my eyes open."

"This is on the second floor?"

"Yes."

"At night?"

"Yes. And then, that night while I slept on the third floor—I'm sure it's my man on the landing. He came up, and why I got scared I don't know because this man is awfully nice, and there is nothing…."

"What do you mean, he came up?"

"I heard him come up the stairs, and he came and watched me."

"Why did you sleep on the third floor that night?"

"Because Roy had turned on the air conditioner. I cannot sleep with an air conditioner."

"So you took one of the guest rooms. Does this room have any particular connection with the landing?"

"You have to go through the landing because of the steps going up and going down. Both end up on the second-floor landing."

"And he came up the stairs, and you felt him standing by your bed?"

"Yes. Watching—probably wondering what I was doing there. But originally this was not a floor used for bedrooms. We did that."

"What was it used for?"

"It was a two-story attic, and we divided it in two by putting in a ceiling, and I don't believe it could have been used except possibly, for servants."

"When was the last time you had a sense of this being?"

"In the fall."

"Is there any particular time when it's stronger?"

"Yes, in the summer."

"Any particular time of day?"

"Dusk."

"Is it always the same person?"

"Well, I always thought it was, but I never gave it too much thought."

"Is there more than one?"

"Yes."

"When did you notice the second 'presence'?"

"It was about two years ago, when Chris, my boy, was moved up to the third floor, that I heard breathing. It was in the master bedroom. I can show you exactly where because the breathing came from the right side of the bed, below, as if a child would have slept in a trundle bed or in a low cradle or something, and that breathing came from below me. The bed is fairly high."

"On the second floor?"

"Yes. And it was very definitely a child, and I can explain that very readily—there is not a mother in the world who will not recognize the breathing of a child, when it's sick and has a fever."

"Did your husband hear this?"

"No. He never hears anything of this."

"But was he present?"

"No. He was in his library, downstairs."

"Was this late at night?"

"No—I go to bed much earlier than Roy. It must have been around eleven, or maybe midnight."

"The first time you heard this, did you wonder what it was?"

"Well, I knew what it was, or what it had to be, since I couldn't possibly hear my children breathe from where I was. I was aware that it must be something which had occurred in that very room before."

"Did you ever hear any other noise?"

"Yes. That child cries, and there is pain."

"How often have you heard it?"

"The breathing more often than the crying. The crying only a couple of times."

"In the same spot?"

"Yes."

"Is there a woman around? Do you have a feeling of a woman when that happens?"

"Yes, and she would be on my side of the bed. And this is the part that bothers me!"

"What do you mean?"

"Because I have the feeling her bed was where mine is. I'm sure she slept on the right, because the child is on the right."

"The furniture in the bedroom is yours—you brought this in yourself?"

"Oh yes, there wasn't anything that belonged to this house."
I thought all this over for a moment, then decided to continue questioning my psychic hostess.

"Was there anything else, other than what we have just discussed?"

"Yes, the portrait of my ancestor that I brought back from France. I was born in 1923, and she was born in 1787."

"And what was her name?"

"I don't remember her maiden name, but she was an Alcazar. She married a Spaniard."

"What is special about the portrait?"

"Of course, the eyes—you will find those eyes in any well-painted portrait—they are eyes that follow you everywhere. But I wouldn't refer to that because this is very common in any museum or in any home where they have family portraits. This is not so much that, but the moods she goes through. She definitely changes her expression. When she disapproves of someone she shows it. And every once in a while, if you glance at her rapidly, she is not the woman you now see in the portrait, but somebody else."

"Does anyone other than you see this?"

"Yes, two other people—my English friend of whom I talked of before, and another English friend who is married to an American friend. They both saw it."

"Have you ever felt anything outside the house, in the grounds?"

"You think there is a branch that's going to hit your face, and yet there is no branch. I thought that people always felt like that when they walked outside, but they don't. Also I can't walk straight in the dark."

"What do you mean?"

"I don't know! I could walk on a straight line, painted line, on the roof without the slightest difficulty, but in the dark I never walk straight."

"You have two dogs. Have they ever behaved strangely?"

"All the time. They bark when there is absolutely nothing there." Mrs. Emery interrupted my thoughtful pause.

"There is also something about a room on this floor, Mr. Holzer."

"The one we're sitting in?"

"No—the next one, where the piano is. Every night before I go to bed I have to have a glass of orange juice. And sometimes I'll race downstairs—I'll feel there is somebody in that rocking chair and I'm afraid to go and check."

"Do you have a feeling of a presence in that room?"

"Yes—oh yes, yes, very strong. Almost every day, I'd say."

"It's that room, and the landing, then?"

"Yes."

At this point I had to change tapes. I thought again about all I had heard and tried to make the various elements fall into place. It didn't seem to add up as yet—at least not in the same time layer.

"To your knowledge," I asked Mrs. Emery, "has anything tragic ever happened here in the house?"

"We don't know. This is the thing that is so disappointing in this country, that so few records are kept. In France you have records for six hundred years. But here, past fifty years people wonder why you want to know."

"Is there any legend, rumor, or tradition attached to the house?"

"There are several legends. They also say that Governor Howard, who gave his name to Howard County, which until 1860 was part of Anne Arundel County, lived in this house. But it's extraordinary, at least to me it is, coming from France, that people cannot be sure of facts which are so recent, really."

"What about the people who lived here before? Have you ever met anybody who lived here before?"

"Yes. I met a man named Talbot Shipley, who is seventy-eight and was born here."

"Did he own the house at one time?"

"His parents did, and—he was the kind, you know, who went, 'Oh! where you have that couch, this is where Aunt Martha was laid out'; and, 'Oh, over there, this is where my mother was when she became an invalid, and this was made into a bedroom and then she died in there'; and, 'Oh, Lynn, you sleep in that room? Well, this is where I was born!' And that's the kind of story we got, but he's a farmer, and he would perhaps not have quite the same conception of a house as we do. To him, a house is where people are born and die. And perhaps to me a house is where people live."

"What about servants? Did you ever have a gardener or anyone working for you?"

"Oh, I have people work for me once in a while. I have discarded all of them because everything is below their dignity and nothing is below mine, so it's much easier to do things myself!"

"Did they ever complain about anything?"

"I had a woman once who said she wouldn't go to the third floor. There is something else," Mrs. Emery said. "There are two niches on either side of where there must have been a triangular porch, which would go with the style of the house. They seem to be sealed. The man who is remodeling the smokehouse into my future antique shop, is dying to open them up and see what's inside them, because really they don't make any sense."

"Do you have any particular feelings about the two niches?"

"They are on each side of my desk on the landing, but on the outside. As a matter of fact, I never thought of that! It's towards the ceiling of the landing but on the outside."

"What could possibly be in them?"

"I don't know. We thought perhaps the records of the house."

"Not a treasure?"

"They say that during the Civil War people buried things, and also during the Revolution, so there could be treasures. Somebody found a coin—1743—on the lane."

"An English coin?"

"Yes."

"Who found it?"

"A young girl who came to see us. So we let her keep it. And a window sill was replaced in the dining room, and quite a few artifacts were found in that window sill. Buttons and coins."

After dinner I went with Mrs. Emery through the house from top to bottom, photographing as I went along. None of the pictures show anything unusual, even in the area of the landing upstairs—but that, of course, does not prove that there is not a presence there lurking for the right moment to be recognized. Only on rare occasions do manifestations of this kind show up on photographic film or paper. It would have taken a great deal more time and patience to come up with positive results.

I talked to the two girls, Ariane and Lynn, now in their early twenties, and to Chris, the little boy, but none of the children had had any unusual experiences as far as the specter on the landing was concerned, nor were they frightened by the prospect of having a ghost or two in the house. It was all part of living in the country. I took a good look at the portrait of the maternal ancestor, and could find only that it was a very good portrait indeed. Perhaps she didn't disapprove of me, or at any rate didn't show it if she did.

But when I stood on the landing, on the spot where most of the manifestations had taken place, I felt rather strange. Granted that I knew where I was and what had occurred in the spot I was standing. Granted also that suggestion works even with professional psychic investigators. There was still a residue of the unexplained. I can't quite put into words what I felt, but it reminded me, in retrospect, of the uneasy feeling I sometimes had when an airplane took a quick and unexpected dive. It is as if your stomach isn't quite where it ought to be. The feeling was passing, but somehow I knew that the spot I had stepped into was not like the rest of the house. I looked around very carefully. Nothing indicated anything special about this landing. The ceiling at this point was not very high, since the available room had been cut in two when the floor was created. But there was a sense of coziness in the area, almost creating an impression of a safe retreat for someone. Could it be then, I reasoned afterwards, that the spectral gentleman had found himself his own niche, his own retreat, and that he very much liked it? Could it not be that he was pleased with the arrangement; that perhaps when the Emerys created an extra floor out of part of the old attic, they had unconsciously carried out the designs of those who had lived in the house before them? Usually hauntings are due to some structural change which does not meet with the approval of those who had lived before in the house. Here we might have the reverse: a later owner doing the bidding of someone who did not have the time or inclination to carry out similar plans. For it must be recalled that a good house is never finished, but lives almost like a human being and thrives on the ministrations of those who truly love it.

It was quite dark outside by now. Nevertheless, I stepped to the nearest window and peered out onto the land below. A sense of calmness came over me, and yet a certain restlessness as if I were expecting something or someone to arrive. Was I picking up the dim vibrations left over from a past event? I don't fancy myself a medium or even remotely psychic, but when I stood on the second floor landing at Howard Lodge, there was a moment when I, too, felt something uncanny within me.

A little later, Roy Emery drove me back to Baltimore and dropped me off at my hotel. Coming back into town was almost like walking into a cold shower, but twenty-four hours later I had again grown accustomed to the rough and materialistic atmosphere of big-city life. I had promised the Emerys to come back someday with a trance medium and see whether I could perhaps let the unknown man on the landing have his say. In the meantime, however, I promised to look up the de Beauregards in France, and Mr. and Mrs. Emery promised to keep me informed of any further developments at Howard Lodge should they occur.

I had hardly returned from Europe when I received an urgent note from Mrs. Emery. On October 20, 1969, she wrote of an incident that had just happened a few weeks before my return.

A friend of mine recently lost her mother and I invited her for the weekend. She was brought here by a mutual friend who also spent the weekend. I was very tired that evening, and shortly before midnight I had to excuse myself. Barbara wanted to stay up and Don stayed with her, feeling that she wanted to talk.

The following morning they told me that they had been sitting in the living room, and that Barbara had turned off the lights because she wanted to enjoy the country peace to the utmost. They then both heard footsteps coming down the steps and assumed that I'd changed my mind and had joined them. They heard the steps cross the threshold and the loveseat creaked under the weight of someone sitting there. Barbara became aware that it was not I there with them, and she could hear someone breathing very regularly. Holding her own breath, she then asked Don if he could hear anything. He had, and had also been holding his breath, to hear better. Barbara and Don both commented on how friendly they felt this presence to be. They are both absolutely convinced that there was someone with them in that room.

It is perhaps a good thing that the unknown gentleman on the second-floor landing does not have to leave his safe retreat to go out into the countryside and search for whatever it is that keeps him on the spot. He would find his beloved countryside vastly changed beyond a few miles. As it is, he can remember it the way he loved it, the way Howard Lodge still reflects it. And the Emerys, far from being upset by the additional inhabitant in their old house, consider it a good omen that someone other than flesh and blood stands guard and peers out, the way a night watchman stands guard over precious property. It assures them of one more pair of eyes and ears should there be something dangerous approaching their house. In this day and age such thoughts are not entirely without reason.

As for the child whose breathing Mrs. Emery heard time and again, we must remember that children died far more often in bygone years than they do today. Child mortality rates were very high because medicine had not yet reached the point where many diseases could be prevented or their death toll sharply reduced. A child then was a far more fragile human being than perhaps it is today. Perhaps it was one of the children belonging to a former owner, who fell ill from a fever and died.

But the gentleman on the landing is another matter. Since it was the lady of the house primarily who felt him and got his attention, I assume that it was a woman who concerned him. Was he, then, looking out from his vantage point to see whether someone were returning home? Had someone left, perhaps, and did part of the gentleman go with her?

One can only surmise such things; there is no concrete evidence whatsoever that it is a gentleman whose lady had left him. Without wishing to romanticize the story, I feel that that may very well have been the case. It is perhaps a bit distressing not to know how to address one's unseen guest other than to call him the "presence on the second-floor landing." But Mrs. Emery knows he is friendly, and that is good enough for her.

14. THE GRAY MAN OF PAWLEY'S ISLAND

One of the best known ghosts of South Carolina's low country is the so-called Gray Man of Pawley's Island. A number of local people claim they have seen him gazing seaward from the dunes, especially when a hurricane is about to break. He is supposed to warn of impending disaster. Who the Gray Man of Pawley's Island is is open to question. According to "A Perceptive Survey of South Carolina Ghosts" by Worth Gatewood, published in 1962, he may be the original Percival Pawley who so loved his island that he felt impelled to watch over it even after he passed on. But Mr. Gatewood gives more credence to a beautiful and romantic account of the origin of the specter. According to this story, a young man who was to be married to a local belle left for New York to attend to some business but on his way back was shipwrecked and lost at sea. After a year's time the young woman married his best friend and settled down on Pawley's Island with her new husband. Years later the original young man returned, again shipwrecked and rescued by one of his former fiancée's servants.

When he realized that his love had married in the meantime, he drowned himself at the nearby shore. All this happened, if we believe it happened, a long time ago, because the Gray Man has been seen ever since 1822, or perhaps even earlier than that. A Mrs. Eileen Weaver, according to Mr. Gatewood's account, saw the specter on her veranda and it was indeed a dim outline of a man in gray. There had been unexplained footsteps on her veranda and doors opening and closing by themselves, untouched by human hands.

A businessman by the name of William Collins who did not believe in ghosts, not even in South Carolina ghosts, found himself on the lookout to check on the rising surf on the morning of famed Hurricane Hazel. As he was walking down the dunes he noticed the figure of a man standing on the beach looking seaward. Collins challenged him, thinking that perhaps he was a neighbor who had come out to check on the rising tide, but the stranger paid no attention. Busy with his task, Collins forgot about this and by the time he looked up the stranger had gone. According to the weather forecast, however, the hurricane had shifted directions and was not likely to hit the area, so Collins and his family went to bed that night, sure the worst was over. At 5 o'clock in the morning he was aroused from bed by heavy pounding on his door. Opening it, he could feel the house shake from the wind rising to tremendous force. On his veranda stood a stranger wearing a gray fishing cap and a common work shirt and pants, all of it in gray. He told Collins to get off the beach since the storm was coming in. Collins thanked him and ran upstairs to wake his family. After the excitement of the storm had passed Collins wondered about the man who had warned him to get off the island. Intelligently he investigated the matter, only to find that no one had seen the man, nor had any of his neighbors had a guest fitting his description. The state highway patrolman on duty also had not seen anyone come or go, and there is only one access road, the causeway over the marshes.

15. THE GHOST OF THE LITTLE WHITE FLOWER

MRS. D. AND HER SON BUCKY lived in a comfortable house on a hilltop in suburban Kentucky, not far from Cincinnati, Ohio, a pleasant, white house, not much different from other houses in the area. The surroundings are lovely and peaceful, and there's a little man-made pond right in front of the house. Nothing about the house or the area looks the least bit ghostly or unusual. Nevertheless Mrs. D. needed my help in a very vexing situation.

Six months after Mrs. D. had moved into the house, she began to hear footsteps upstairs when there was no one about, and the sound of a marble being rolled across the hall. Anything supernatural was totally alien to Mrs. D.

Nevertheless, Mrs. D. had a questioning and alert mind, and was not about to accept these phenomena without finding out what caused them. When the manifestations persisted, she walked up to the foot of the stairs and yelled, "Why don't you just come out and show yourself or say something instead of making all those noises?"

As if in answer, an upstairs door slammed shut and then there was utter silence. After a moment's hesitation, Mrs. D. dashed upstairs and made a complete search. There was no one about and the marble, which seemingly had rolled across the floor, was nowhere to be seen.

When the second Christmas in the new house rolled around, the D.s were expecting Bucky home from the Army. He was going to bring his sergeant and the sergeant's wife with him, since they had become very friendly. They celebrated New Year's Eve in style and high spirits (not the ethereal kind, but the bottled type). Nevertheless, they were far from inebriated when the sergeant suggested that New Year's Eve was a particularly suitable night for a séance. Mrs. D. would have no part of it at first. She had read all about phony séances and such, and remembered what her Bible said about such matters. Her husband had long gone to bed. The four of them decided to have a go at it. They joined hands and sat quietly in front of the fireplace. Nothing much happened for a while. Then Bucky, who had read some books on psychic phenomena, suggested that they needed a guide or control from the other side of life to help them, but no one had any suggestions concerning to whom they might turn. More in jest than as a serious proposal, Mrs. D. heard herself say, "Why don't you call your Indian ancestor Little White Flower!" Mr. D. is part Cherokee, and Bucky, the son would, of course, consider this part of his inheritance too. Mrs. D. protested that all this was nonsense, and that they should go to bed. She assured them that nothing was likely to happen. But the other three were too busy to reply, staring behind her into the fireplace. When she followed the direction of their eyes she saw what appeared to be some kind of light similar to that made by a flashlight. It stayed on for a short time and then disappeared altogether.

From that day on Mrs. D. started to find strange objects around the house that had not been there a moment before. They were little stones in the shape of Indian arrows. She threw them out as fast as she found them. Several weeks later, when she was changing the sheets on her bed, she noticed a huge red arrow had been painted on the bottom sheet—by unseen hands.

It was in the winter of 1963. One afternoon she was lying down on the couch with a book trying to rest. Before long she was asleep. Suddenly she awoke with a feeling of horror which seemed to start at her feet and gradually work its way up throughout her entire body and mind. The room seemed to be permeated with something terribly evil. She could neither see nor hear anything, but she had the feeling that there was a presence there and that it was very strong and about to overcome her.

For a few weeks she felt quite alone in the house, but then things started up again. The little stone arrowheads appeared out of nowhere again all over the house. Hysterical with fear, Mrs. D. called upon a friend who had dabbled in metaphysics and asked for advice. The friend advised a séance in order to ask Little White Flower to leave.

Although Little White Flower was not in evidence continuously and seemed to come and go, Mrs. D. felt the woman's influence upon her at all times. Later the same week, Little White Flower put in another appearance, this time visual. It was toward 4 o'clock in the morning when Mrs. D. woke up with the firm impression that her tormentor was in the room. As she looked out into the hall, she saw on the wall a little red object resembling a human eye, and directly below it what seemed like half a mouth. Looking closer, she discerned two red eyes and a white mouth below. It reminded her of some clowns she had seen in the circus. The vision remained on the wall for two or three minutes, and then vanished completely.

After several postponements I was finally able to come to Kentucky and meet with Mrs. D. in person. On June 20, 1964, I sat opposite the slightly portly, middle-aged lady who had corresponded with me for several months so voluminously.

As I intoned my solemn exorcism and demanded Little White Flower's withdrawal from the spot, I could hear Mrs. D. crying hysterically. It was almost as if some part of her was being torn out and for a while it seemed that she was being sent away, not Little White Flower.

The house has been quiet ever since; Little White Flower has presumably gone back to her own people and Mrs. D. continues living in the house without further disturbances.